BECOMING

Spiritual Soulmates

WITH YOUR

Child

Becoming

Spiritual

Soulmates

WITH YOUR

Child

ROBERT & DEBRA BRUCE

BROADMAN
& HOLMAN
PUBLISHERS

Nashville, Tennessee

Published by
Broadman & Holman Publishers
Nashville, Tennessee

Design: Leslie Joslin

4262-69
0-8054-6269-4

Dewey Decimal Classification: 649
Subject Heading: PARENTING \ CHILD REARING \ CHRISTIAN GROWTH
Library of Congress Card Catalog Number: 95-46558

Unless noted otherwise, Scriptures are taken from the TLB, The Living Bible, copyright © Tyndale House Publishers, Wheaton, Ill., 1971, used by permission. Verses also are taken from the NRSV, New Revised Standard Version of the Bible, copyright © 1989 by the Division of Christian Education of the National Council of Churches of Christ in the United States of America, used by permission, all rights reserved; and RSV, Revised Standard Version of the Bible, copyrighted 1946, 1952, © 1971, 1973.

Library of Congress Cataloging-in-Publication Data
Bruce, Robert G., 1949–.
    Becoming spiritual soulmates with your child / Robert and Debra Bruce.
        p.   cm.
    Includes bibliographical references.
    ISBN 0-8054-6269-4 (pbk.)
    1. Christian education—Home training. 2. Children—Religious life.
    3. Parenting—Religious aspects—Christianity. 4. Children—Conversion to
    Christianity. I. Bruce, Debra Fulghum, 1951– . II. Title.
        BV1590.B78   1996
        268'.432—dc20
        95-46558
        CIP
        AC
        00 99 98 97 96 5 4 3 2 1

To Our Spiritual Soulmates
Rob, Brittnye, and Ashley

Contents

Acknowledgments

With heartfelt thanks, we acknowledge the following for their intimate involvement and participation in this book.

Jewel Holden Fulghum
Robert G. Bruce III
Brittnye Holden Bruce
Ashley Elizabeth Bruce
Linda McIlwain
Rev. Henry Steinmeyer
Ellen Oldacre, editor
ParentLife magazine editorial staff
Living with Teenagers magazine editorial staff
Christian Parenting Today magazine editorial staff
Home Life magazine editorial staff
Janis Whipple, Broadman & Holman editor

Foreword

I thought it was just going to be another ordinary afternoon car ride with my three-year-old (and recently potty-trained) daughter and her seven-year-old brother. Silly me! From somewhere out of the blue—and my son's theological mind—came the question, "Mom, will there be any toys in heaven?"

Now I was semi-prepared to answer questions on salvation or even the Trinity, but "toys in heaven" was not on my "ready" list. I think our kids must go to some sort of school before birth that teaches them to ask us the exact questions we aren't prepared to answer. But I put on my expert parenting face and answered, "Stuart, heaven will be a place where we are always happy because Jesus is there and all our needs will be taken care of."

"I know that, Mom, but I just didn't know if that meant toys," Stuart responded.

I continued, "Son, if you think you will need toys, then God will take care of your needs." (Before you critique the theological soundness of that answer, you have to be sure you know, beyond a shadow of a doubt, that there won't be any toys there!)

Our continued conversation on the all-inclusiveness of heaven was gently interrupted by a forgotten three-year-old, Emily, in the back seat, who asked, "Mommy, will there be potties too?"

Now toys are important; but to Emily, bathrooms took priority. I assured her that God would take care of her needs; and if she needed a potty, then it would be there. That seemed to satisfy her.

I am constantly amazed by the ways God uses our children to help us understand His love and plan for us. That day, God reminded me that He will always meet my needs, even if it's just in knowing how to respond to my children's spiritual questions. Assuring my children that all our needs will be met in heaven allowed me to assure them that God takes care of us every day.

Becoming spiritual soulmates with your child is not easy. Sometimes I work so hard at rearing spiritual children that I make it a job instead of a calling. I choose to be a "mommy martyr" instead of choosing to trust God to meet our needs. That's when I begin to spend all my energy protecting my kids from the world, instead of helping them learn how to make choices that honor God and help others.

We can't give our kids what we don't have. Christian author Josh McDowell says, "You can con a con and fool a fool, but you cannot kid a kid." If I'm not a godly person, then I won't be a godly wife—and I certainly won't be a godly mother. No matter how many times I go to church, serve on committees, feed the poor, or attend a Bible study, I can't "earn" my godliness. If I don't completely trust all that I am and all I want my family to be to God, then I have lied to my children.

We no longer live in a town, state, or nation where the majority of the population desires to be godly. Yet our children must understand that only a loving, almighty God can meet all our needs. Their understanding will come only through our modeling.

Robert and Debra Bruce have three children. They understand parent panic and family frustration. They write from a wealth of personal experience as parents and as Christians. This book will give you some very practical handles to grab and immediately put into practice.

Just reading this book will not get the job done, but it can provide a new beginning. It can help you rediscover—or discover for the first time—the God of peace. He is the ultimate parental role model, and He is waiting to be invited on our parenting journey. So whether you are worried about toys or potties, allow Him to meet your needs.

Ellen Oldacre,
editor of *ParentLife*
and *Living with Teenagers* magazines

Introduction

Sharing God in a Secular Society

On a hot summer night more than twenty-one years ago at Emory University Hospital in Atlanta, we were honored with the titles of "Mom" and "Dad." Rob, our firstborn son, came into the world with mighty screams as he told boldly of his presence. Later that morning we stood with Deb's father, staring through the newborn nursery window, admiring this newest miracle of God's love and our love. As we joined the ranks of billions of parents before us, this wise gentleman challenged us to accountability. "God has blessed you with a perfect child," he said. "What becomes of him now depends on you."

What would become of him? Of his siblings? That night we made a commitment to God, to each other, and to our children to be the *very best parents we could be*. It hasn't always been easy, for we have learned there are profound differences between being a parent and being a Christian parent.

We believe that being a Christian parent means making time each day to:

- share God's love with our children,

- acknowledge God's presence in everyday life, and

- teach the message of salvation with faith in God as the expected result.

IT STARTS WITH ACCOUNTABILITY

You see, as Christian parents, we represent the incarnate love of Jesus Christ to our children. What becomes of them really does depend on us, and it starts with our *accountability* and *commitment* to be the dedicated leaders of a Christ-centered home.

Since you are reading this book, you probably feel as we do about being a parent. We would go to the ends of the earth to protect Rob, Brittnye, and Ashley. We've worked hard to give them healthful meals, good medical care, and suitable clothing. They enjoy a comfortable home in a safe community, attend excellent schools and colleges, and are active in our neighborhood church. When they were young and vulnerable, we screened their friends, handpicked their teachers, coached their teams, chaperoned their field trips, and intervened if we felt anyone or anything was a negative influence. We wanted to protect our precious children from any opposing influence in our secular society.

In the midst of trying to give our children every opportunity in life, however, we can become so overwhelmed by the tangible that we forget about the most important aspect of human development—*spirituality*. And spiritual maturity is a key factor in how we cope with the trials and tribulations of this earthly life.

As today's family faces many intrusions—extracurricular activities, school, church or business meetings at night, long work hours or business travel, neighbors and teachers who are not Christians—parents must *make time daily* to nurture a child's spiritual development.

WHAT IS SPIRITUAL DEVELOPMENT?

Spiritual development is the growth of a child's view of the world. It is the process by which children form a Christian perspective about their families and themselves. Like sexual or cognitive development, spiritual development is a natural process that unfolds spontaneously if a child is supported and encouraged. When it is suppressed or inhibited, however, a child is neither adequately equipped to confront religious questions nor sufficiently secure to get the most out of life.[1]

To equip our three children spiritually, we hold fast to the truth found in Proverbs 22:6, NRSV: "Train children in the right way, and when old, they will not stray." Using this Scripture as a foundation for our parenting, we have written this book as a training guide for parents—to help you zero in on the diverse aspects of spiritual discipline in the Christian home. We feel it is important for you to understand your role as parent, teacher, and spiritual guide; and we have provided you with innovative suggestions to help make this a reality.

Simply stated, spirituality reclaims that part of life—all too often disowned—that represents faith and imagination. If we help children cultivate that impulse, they will retain their spontaneity and sense of spiritual exhilaration in years to come.[2] As parents you can enable the child's spiritual life to blossom as you take her on an intimate, soul-searching journey. Your child's self-worth will grow as you:

- practice what you preach and role model spirituality;
- take a faith inventory and check your "internal" life;
- share a personal faith in our Lord Jesus Christ;
- get involved in a local church—together;
- read the Bible with your child, explain how the Scriptures are meaningful today, and encourage a daily prayer time;
- teach your child to look for God's love in all people and in all things each day;
- teach your child the importance of an active prayer life;

- go beyond teaching values by showing your child how to follow ways of love demonstrated by Jesus Christ;

- root your child in the Christian faith so that when he faces life's opposing influences, he has protection;

- encourage your child when she has doubts;

- let your child know that eternal life is the hope of our faith; and

- show your child how to "put feet to faith."

WE HAVE LOST OUR SOCIAL NETWORK

Remember when you were a child? Who taught you about God? Who helped ignite that spiritual yearning in your soul? We both agree that our parents helped us to develop a spiritual life; but we also have great memories of singing hymns with our extended family—grandparents, aunts, uncles, and cousins—as they also played a fundamental role in reinforcing our belief and value system. Debra recalls numerous childhood trips to Aunt Julia's ranch and worshiping in church with aunts, uncles, and cousins. She didn't know many in the congregation, but hearing the singing of familiar hymns gave Deb a comforting sense of security and well-being. Bob's grandmother lived with the family during his childhood. Grandma Bruce would spend hours reading Bible stories to him and his sisters and praying with them nightly.

Such memories are rare for many children today. In the midst of our transient society, we have lost our social network. Perhaps this lack of family support is one reason for the growing need for spirituality in America today. In years past, people lived close to family members and relied on parents and siblings for affirmation, empathy, and emotional strength—even after marriage. When suffering occurred, people could turn to relatives for comfort and support. Yet in our highly mobile society, many adults today live hundreds of miles away from parents and siblings.

Why is this social support so important for spiritual development? *Close relationships with family and friends allow us to nourish our hungry souls.* When we are tied emotionally to those we love, we can let go of bottled-up feelings of fear, insecurity, and guilt, and receive comfort from people who accept us just as we are. If we have no place where we feel safe enough to let down our emotional defenses, then our guard tends to remain up all the time—a guard that masks the very troubles we face.

SPIRITUAL DEVELOPMENT BEGINS AT HOME

In a transient and secular society, if our children are to develop spiritual strength and continue the legacy of the Christian faith, then parents must lead the way through spiritual discipline at home.

You may say: "I don't know how to share my faith. I can't even recite Scriptures. Can I still be my child's spiritual guide?"

To that we say a resounding *yes.* Rearing a spiritual child in the Christian faith extends far beyond reciting Scriptures. In his book, *Talking to Your Child about God,* psychologist David Heller says that "the greatest gift you can give your child is the gift of soul—a set of values and understandings with which to view the world."[3] Spiritual training, along with biblical knowledge, helps to secure them.

As our middle daughter, Brittnye, completed her freshman year in college, she called us late one night to say, "Thank you." "I just want you to know that I'm going to bring my children up just like you did—in the church," she shared. "When I look around the dorm and at my friends, the people with a strong personal faith in God are the ones who can handle the ups and downs of college life."

Brittnye's keen observation illustrates the truth that children and teens who are anchored by a steadfast faith in God feel more secure and are able to go into peer situations equipped with higher self-esteem and moral tenacity. As Brittnye witnessed, when children become "connected" with God, their self-esteem increases, they are able to see the goodness in others, and, most importantly, they are able to cope with the hard knocks and disappointments that come in their young lives—and they will come!

FAITH BOOSTS SELF-ESTEEM

Think back to when you accepted Christ into your life. Remember how your confidence soared and how burdens that once seemed so great became bearable in the arms of God's love? Self-esteem is vital for all of us. As our children grow in faith, they are better able to love themselves, love others, and love God. What other strengths can occur as their spirituality develops muscle?

- She will cope more easily with the ups and downs of life.

- He is more likely to attract others who have healthy self-esteem. Children with low self-esteem seek other low self-esteem children; we are naturally drawn to others with a similar sense of self-regard.

- She will think about what she wants out of life, will be more ambitious in going after it, and will be more likely to achieve it.

- He will find it easier to confront obstacles, fears, and interpersonal conflicts rather than avoid them, and to solve problems instead of worrying over them. The child with low self-esteem sees problems as grounds for saying, "I quit."

- She will try to find ways to get along with others and to be helpful.

- He will feel more secure, friendly, trusting, cheerful, and optimistic.

- She will be able to value her achievements without a constant need for approval from others. Self-worth is not dependent on outside forces putting a stamp of approval on our work and accomplishments.

- He will begin to take responsibility for his actions and be willing to challenge himself.[4]

SHARE FROM THE EYES OF YOUR SOUL

Children begin learning about our faith from infancy, as they are held close by loving Christian mothers and fathers. Even a newborn can sense the love of God through a parent's gentle touch. Starting as early as the toddler years, parents can encourage the disciplines of faith by teaching their child a devotional habit; by talking about Jesus Christ with the child so he can learn to see God in daily experiences; by sharing a personal faith "from the eyes of your soul"; and by handling doubts the child may have when he deals with fear or failure.

In short, the ultimate goal for the Christian parent in the nineties is quite clear: to send a child into a very turbulent, secular society—knowing that he can stand strong on his personal beliefs in our Lord and Savior Jesus Christ.

As you make this your parenting goal, remember this: "God is love, and those who abide in love abide in God, and God abides in them" (1 John 4:16b, NRSV). As the leader of your home, remind yourself that you may be the best Christian your child knows. That is an awesome but realistic concept we all must comprehend. Understanding the importance of our actions and words in a child's eyes gives us even more reason to watch what we say and do—because she watches what we say and do!

To get started nurturing your child's spiritual development, pray daily that God will prepare the heart of your child to accept the message of salvation. Look for opportunities to share what your faith means to you *from the eyes of your soul.* After all, don't we all remember what touches our heart? Your child can experience God's love in a whole new way as you tell him about God's saving grace and how a personal relationship with His Son, Jesus Christ, can open doors to new life. Gently steer your child toward the good news of Jesus Christ without making it a power struggle.

LEAN ON THE "E-FACTOR"

In essence, the key to nurturing your child's spirituality lies in what we call "the E-factor"—being *enthusiastic* about your own faith. *Enthusiasm* means "filled with God," and enthusiasm about your Christian faith is contagious. If your attitude toward God is one of joy and anticipation each day, your child will pattern his concept of the Christian faith that way too. One of our most rewarding affirmations came from our son, Rob, when he was trying to get a friend to accompany him to a youth fellowship in high school: "Hey, being a Christian is awesome. You never know what God has in store for you each day!"

What does God have in store for you today? For your children? Now more than ever before, your child's spiritual development is the most significant step in his growth. You can instill a passion for God and spiritual awareness in your child without taking extraordinary measures if you begin with your own commitment.

Paul laid down a challenge worthy of our consideration: "Standing side by side with one strong purpose—to tell the Good News" (Phil. 1:27b). This is the message for parents today as we stand accountable for spiritual training.

DOES JESUS CHRIST LIVE IN YOUR HOME?

How do you become a spiritual soulmate with your child? There are no easy answers. It takes commitment, time, and an ongoing prayer relationship with your heavenly Father. Start by checking your internal life, then take the faith inventory shown on pages 23 and 24. Begin to work on the areas indicated in your own spiritual life. Thank God for coming into your life and for giving you special gifts and talents. It is only by strengthening these—and your *internal life*—that you begin to help your child develop spiritually. As you feel a spiritual awareness of the presence of the living Lord, let this spirituality *enthusiastically* pour into your family's daily activities. In each chapter you will find innovative activities and suggestions for you and your child on how to ingrain spiritual values into daily living. Most importantly, allow Jesus Christ to live in your home as you seek His guidance for your goals, personal decisions, and family direction.

There is an old story about a husband who came home from work. He asked his wife, "Did anything happen today?"

She answered, "Well, the pastor came by for prayer, and he asked me a question. He asked, 'Does Jesus Christ live here?'"

The husband indignantly responded, "Did you tell him that we have been members of the church for thirty years?"

She replied, "Yes, dear, but that's not what the pastor asked."

"Did you tell him that I am among the largest givers to his church?" the husband responded, growing angry.

"But that's not what he asked," she answered. "He asked, 'Does Jesus Christ live here?'"

Does Jesus Christ live in your home? Have you asked Him to join your family? To live in your heart? In the hearts of your children? It is our heartfelt prayer that this book will help make a difference in your life and the lives of your children. As we write this, we are praying for a new beginning for each one of you and your families as you take steps to get acquainted with our living Lord and make spiritual training a daily routine in your homes.

Anthony Campolo, a renowned Christian sociologist and author of *It's Friday, but Sunday's Coming,* tells about a sociological study in which fifty people over the age of ninety-five were asked one question: "If you could live your life over again, what would you do differently?" It was an open-ended question, and it produced a multiplicity of answers. However, three answers constantly reemerged and dominated the results of the study:

- If I had it to do over again, I would reflect more.

- If I had it to do over again, I would risk more.

- If I had it to do over again, I would do more things that would live on after I am gone.

IT'S NOT TOO LATE!

If you commit yourself to following the practices taught in this book, you won't have to worry whether it's too late to reflect on the meaning of your faith and your spiritual journey. Starting today, you can reach out in love and teach your child about a life-changing relationship with our Lord and Savior Jesus Christ. You can leave a legacy that will last long after you are gone—a firm, spiritual foundation that will carry your child through this life . . . into eternal life.

What spiritual changes need to be made in your home? In your personal life? Let the following pages challenge you to create an environment in your home where spirituality is tenderly nurtured and God's empowering love is shared.

SPIRITUAL FOOD FOR THOUGHT

1. What role do your extended family members—grandparents, aunts, uncles, and cousins—play in reinforcing the belief and value system that you teach? How can you involve these family members to support your teachings as you nurture spirituality in your child?

2. Spiritual training can take place on common ground in the home—while washing dishes with your teen, picking up toys with your toddler, or raking leaves with your child. Where is the common ground in your home for sharing your faith in Jesus Christ? Make an effort this week to discover

this common ground as you tell your child about faith in God.

3. What effect does modern technology have in your home? Does it keep your family from communicating? From talking about your faith? Make plans this week to get control of the TV, video games, and computer as you meet your children on common ground.

4. Does Jesus live in your home? If Jesus were to come to your home today, would He know you are Christians? What changes would you need to make internally and externally to exemplify the Christian faith? Take time this week to decorate your child's room with pictures of Jesus, scenes from the Bible, or contemporary posters that illustrate favorite Scriptures. Make sure that the Bible is centrally located in your home so that all who enter may know that yours is a Christ-centered family.

5. Enthusiasm means being "filled with God." How enthusiastic are you about your faith? What would help you get more excited? As you talk about God in your home this week, try to do so with more enthusiasm. Does this "E-factor" make a difference in how you are received?

One

How's Your Internal Life?

After months of bringing his children to Sunday School and church, Paul, the father of two elementary-school-age girls, shared his concern that his children wouldn't pray at bedtime. "I tell them to say their prayers," he told us, "but they say they don't want to. What can I do to encourage them?"

"Do you ever pray in front of them?" we asked. "What about at bedtime? Do you pray with them?"

Paul shook his head to both questions. "No, they've never seen me pray."

We find it interesting that many devoted Christian parents buy books about spiritual development, make sure their children go to church each week, and purchase expensive Bibles for them. Yet when it comes to praying, sharing their faith, or bonding spiritually with their children and the Lord, these same parents hesitate.

Becoming spiritual soulmates with your child depends on this: All the talk about spiritual development in your home won't make a difference unless you lead the way. Telling your child to read her Bible, go to church, pray at night, and spend time listening to God is in vain—unless you are modeling the same activities.

That's like telling your child to eat his spinach when you never eat yours, or telling him not to watch television when you constantly sit in front of the set.

The exciting news is that reading this book indicates you have made a commitment to start your child on his unique spiritual journey. Yet before you can begin teaching your child about a personal relationship with Jesus Christ and a daily "walk of wonder" with God, you need to do some homework.

START WITH A PERSONAL SPIRITUAL COMMITMENT

In our own lives, nurturing spirituality in our children has been a challenge. We must constantly evaluate our personal commitment to Jesus Christ and strive to live in love as He taught. With Bob as the senior pastor of a large church and Debra as a Christian author, you might assume we have all the credentials to develop a child's spiritual nature. The truth is that no matter what your educational background or career is, no matter how strong your prayer life or Bible knowledge is, no matter how often you attend church, you must first look internally—to the eyes of your soul—before you can nurture spiritual development in your child. As much as we try to encourage spiritual development in our home, we still face work diversions, family interruptions, and exhausted minds and bodies from time to time—all stopping us from guiding our children in the manner of God's Holy Word.

We have written this book because we believe that *nothing we do in life is more important than to grow spiritually—from the inside out*. When we acknowledge our inner spirit, our soul, we begin to embrace the true character of our being—the essence of who we are. Only then are we able to tackle life's demands with greater enthusiasm (remember the "E-factor" shared in the introduction?). Spiritual fulfillment has always been available for everyone, but we must allow this realization to become a vital part of our life today, and we are the ones who must enthusiastically teach our children about spiritual wholeness.

It's ironic that for most of us, seeking spiritual wholeness and actually finding it are two different issues. We say we want to be spiritual people and know God, but we often don't know how. We aren't entirely sure what to make of such notions as spirituality, transformation, or conversion. We're turned off by one televangelist, yet tantalized by another. We're surrounded by self-help books and spiritual psychology, but don't know where to dig in. From glitzy religious shows we hear stories of dramatic conversions, but we suspect sham. We wistfully toy with techniques that relax us and promise us abundant health, wealth, and a happy home. Yet in the end, we find ourselves straining for a deeper sense of spiritual assurance, inner peace, and unqualified grace.[1]

START WITH TRADITION

In our years of ministry in the local church—and of parenting—we have observed that tradition is a mighty force in the lives of most Christians as they seek a deeper sense of inner peace. Tradition influences our worship, our celebrations, the way we conduct our careers, and the way we judge what is acceptable behavior in all of life. From time to time, people in our culture have sought to liberate themselves from the shackles of tradition as they understood it, but they have met with limited success. We believe that tradition helps us discover meaning in our lives. It helps give form and substance to life. We are not creators of a brave new world at all; we are but builders on foundations already laid by generations of thoughtful and courageous men and women who came before us. In fact, the power of tradition is one of the things that has helped our Christian faith abide for 2,000 years!

The problem occurs when we become such zealous keepers of religious traditions that we never encounter God. Thousands upon thousands of people faithfully attend church. They have stars for

15

perfect attendance in Sunday School and tithe generously. Yet many have never really come to grips with the two great commandments of Scripture: "Thou shalt love the Lord thy God with all thy heart, and with all thy soul, and with all thy mind . . . and love thy neighbor as thyself" (Matt. 23:37–39, KJV).

THEN MOVE BEYOND TRADITION

To become spiritual soulmates with their children, parents must move beyond reliance on the great traditions and lean on their "internal" life and their personal relationship with Jesus Christ.

One of the important rituals of the Jewish people was ceremonial washing. This law was not a matter of hygiene as much as it was of ceremony. The Pharisees—indeed all devout Jews—would not eat unless they had washed their hands in a particular way. They had other traditions concerning the washing of cups, pots, and tables. It must have been quite unsettling to the Pharisees to see Jesus' disciples ignore these rituals. To put this in perspective, we might get the same kind of feeling if a guest at our table began eating immediately without waiting for all to be served or for the blessing. There would be a certain awkwardness—a feeling that something sacred had been violated. Since the Pharisees were well-known for their devotion to tradition, their feeling of violation must have been particularly acute.

"Why do your disciples disobey the ancient Jewish traditions?" they asked Jesus. "For they ignore our ritual of ceremonial hand-washing before they eat" (Matt. 15:2).

"You hypocrites!" Jesus responded, "You teach man-made laws instead of those from God" (Matt. 15:7–9).

Sometimes Jesus seemed unduly harsh with the Pharisees. They seemed to be asking a reasonable question. Perhaps Jesus knew that for the Pharisees to open themselves anew and afresh to God, radical surgery would be necessary. Remember how He told Nicodemus that he would have to be born all over again to enter the kingdom of God? His harshness must have been a desperate attempt to shake them out of their lethargy so that He might reveal to them the tradition-shattering truth about God.

FOCUS ON MATTERS OF THE HEART

That can happen to Christians today too. We can get so attached to the external trappings of religion—to the traditions of our faith—that we miss the heart of the matter. But it doesn't have to be this way. You and your children can experience a deeper truth. To do that, we want you to take your attention off the power of tradition for awhile and focus instead on Jesus' teaching about the external and the internal. It's not what a man was on the outside that mattered to Jesus, but what he was on the inside.

This is an important lesson for each of us—a lesson that we as parents must learn, then teach to our children. Think about it. Aren't secular matters—how we look, what we wear, the automobile we drive, the neighborhood we live in, our upwardly mobile careers, or educational degrees—more important to most of us than what our spiritual life is or should be?

The problem is that when we focus only on secular matters, we lose sight of matters of the heart. We forget an essential teaching of our faith: That which is external deteriorates and decays in time, but that which is internal is eternal. Our inner selves determine our destiny, and it is this inner spirit that we must nourish each day.

EMPHASIZE THE INNER PERSON

Let's consider three reasons why we need to place a renewed emphasis on the internal, on the spiritual, in our lives:

Spirituality Helps Give Life Meaning

We need a new emphasis on our spiritual lives to prevent an existence that's all glitter with no real substance. Many people today are ambitious, well-educated, and financially successful, but how many of us experience loneliness and a nagging lack of purpose or inner peace? Millions are reportedly seeking a "higher power" in their lives. One *U.S. News and World Report* poll found that 93 percent of those surveyed believed in God or a universal spirit, and 76 percent of Americans questioned said that God was a heavenly Father who could be reached through prayer.

Psychotherapist James Hillman was one of the first to rediscover the soul as an important concept in psychotherapy. Yet it was Thomas Moore, one of Hillman's followers, who identified "soul-sickness" as an epidemic sweeping our planet. "Emptiness; meaninglessness; vague depression; disillusionment about marriage, family, relationships; a loss of values; yearning for personal fulfillment; a hunger for spirituality" are symptoms Moore identifies when people "lose the soul."[2]

If you are like most people today, you are overwhelmed by the frantic pace of life. Perhaps you admit to being caught up in the whirlwind of runaway schedules, careers that take precedence over personal needs, nonstop carpooling, volunteer commitments, unruly children, rebellious teens, nightly fast food, and no time for self.

The problem with living such an overly committed life is this: in the midst of hurried and often meaningless days, you ignore spiritual needs. While you may intellectually understand that an orderly life and sense of direction are both vital to your overall well-being, the demands you face each day make both difficult to attain.

Many people tell of being emotionally hungry as they search for deeper spiritual roots in life. This quest for spirituality is not just another psychological fad or trendy pursuit for the nineties; it is based on a deep-seated inner need. This need is growing; people crave spiritual fulfillment and inner strength to face the multiple challenges of life.

Has this emptiness led to the documented spiritual revival in America today? We think so! We don't believe it was just a coincidence that William Bennett's *The Book of Virtues,* climbed to the top of the bestseller list—pushing aside such popular books as Howard Stern's shocking autobiography.

Princeton Religion Research Center reported a recent Gallup poll that validates the fact that America has hit rock bottom and is now searching for "spiritual moorings." As evidence, George Gallup notes:

- 40 percent of Americans meet weekly in small groups for caring and sharing, and another 7 percent want to join;

- the media are beginning to realize the importance of religion;

- psychiatry no longer dismisses the importance of religious faith in recovery from emotional illness;

- the connection between prayer and healing is increasingly acknowledged;

- researchers are beginning to focus on the inner life;

- three out of four people recognize selfishness as a serious problem in America;

- some in Hollywood are struggling to produce moral and spiritually uplifting films such as *Forrest Gump;*

- new efforts are under way to teach character and religious values in the classroom;

- statistics show people with a religious orientation have a 47 percent lower high-school dropout rate and are 54 percent less likely to use drugs.[3]

We believe the masses have spoken: America is still a religious nation, and spiritual longing is skyrocketing.

Spirituality Gives Life Protection

We need to strengthen our spiritual lives as protection against being crushed by life's harsher realities. One reason the fitness craze is so strong is that it gives us a sense of control over our lives. Many psychologists say that the greatest fear for many of us is having lack of control, so we work very hard to establish ourselves in our work and in the accumulation of things.

Then we can sit back and say to ourselves: "I am in control of my destiny."

Yet life is rarely that simple. There are peaks and valleys. Warm, hope-filled days let us bask in a friendly and peaceful glow, but then comes the storms that rake and ravage mercilessly. Just when we think we have life just the way we want it, we face life's interruptions: the death of a spouse, the loss of a job, the disruption of a marriage, the onset of a serious illness. Where do we find the resources to cope?

Going back to our traditions does help. Studies have shown that people who have learned the great prayers of the church or who have steeped themselves in Scripture find tremendous comfort. Nevertheless, it is not the prayers or the passages of Scripture themselves that comfort; it is our God who speaks to us through them.

Where do we find the strength to deal with life's harshest blows? We find it by building up our inner strength. Paul wrote in 1 Timothy 4:8, "Bodily exercise is all right, but spiritual exercise is much more important and is a tonic for all you do. So exercise yourself spiritually and practice being a better Christian, because that will help you not only now in this life, but in the next life too."

Just as we can build up our outer body by regular and consistent exercise, so we can strengthen our inner resources by consistent cultivation of our relationship with God.

Spirituality Prepares Us for Eternity

Spiritual strength will help us prevent moral weakness. It will give us protection against personal crises. Yet we need to strengthen our spiritual lives for a third reason: as preparation for an eternity in the presence of God.

Remember the external/internal principle? Everything external deteriorates and decays. Only that which we are on the inside remains. When we are searching for the perfect school for our child, the sheltered neighborhood to purchase our home, or the safest car to drive, we first need to ask ourselves: What are we doing to strengthen our spiritual life and that of our children? What are we doing to prepare for eternal life with our Lord Jesus Christ?

Ralph Waldo Emerson said, "What lies behind us and what lies before us are tiny matters compared to what lies within us." He was merely stating for the modern world what Jesus Christ taught two thousand years ago: we must strengthen our spiritual life, our internal life, to find meaning in this hurried world.

When our daughter Brittnye was five years old, she recited John 3:16 as follows: "For God so loved the world that he gave his only begotten Son, that whosoever believeth in him, should not perish but have *internal* life." Out of the mouths of babes! How is your internal life?

Now Take Steps toward Salvation

We have experienced that the best model for parenting is God, the Father, who offers you unconditional love through Jesus Christ. This is the type of love we will challenge you to follow in your families.

As the leader in your home, you can take steps right now toward a saving personal relationship with Jesus Christ. The following Scriptures will help you discover what the Bible says about new life in Christ.

1. God loves you: John 3:16 and 10:10.

2. You are a sinner in need of forgiveness: Romans 3:23 and 6:23.

3. God wants to forgive you: Romans 5:8 and 1 Peter 3:18.

4. You must turn away from your sins: Luke 13:5 and Ephesians 2:8–9.

5. You must place your faith in God's Son: Jesus Christ, Acts 20:21 and John 14:6.

PLACE YOUR FAITH IN JESUS

As you take steps to strengthen your internal life, admit to God that you are a sinner and are turning away from your sins. Place your belief in Jesus Christ; then commit your life to Him as you ask Him to be your Lord and Savior.[4]

Once you have made (or renewed) your commitment to Christ, it's time to nurture your personal faith and help your child in his spiritual walk with the Lord. A parent's role is vital. Since you are the interpreter of your child's significant life experiences and the adviser on her difficult questions, you are also your child's most influential guide to religious beliefs, practices, and the spiritual process.[5]

Realizing the importance of a parent's actions and words in a child's eyes gives us even more reason to keep watch over our internal lives. When we're filled with turmoil and helpless frustration, we pass it on to our children.

REEXAMINE YOUR LIFE'S DIRECTION

As you make a commitment to Jesus Christ and to spiritual development in the home, reexamine your internal life. Each day God gives us opportunities to reexamine our direction and purpose. Life is full of these kinds of moments. In the normal course of events, they introduce a sobering "wake-up" thought to our minds, no matter how shallow our life may be.

One of these times comes when we are ill. We wonder about pain, why we were born, and what death will be like. When we leave home, we discover another time for reflection. Who am I without my family? Does God live everywhere? When we get married and become parents, we have a multitude of inner questions:

What kind of husband or wife will I be? What kind of father or mother will I become? Am I all that I want to be? Should I change what I have been? If so, how?

The entire maturing process gears us toward self-examination—from childhood and adolescence through young adulthood and to middle and old age.

These are God-given opportunities—not to be feared nor ignored, but to be grasped and used for our personal and spiritual growth. Someone has rightly said that the unexamined life is not worth living!

The good news that we want to emphasize in this book is that *we don't have to be perfect, but we should be striving and moving in the direction of Christ.* We are the body of Christ on this earth, and it is this message that we must teach our children.

TAKE A FAITH INVENTORY

Take the following Faith Inventory, and see where your strengths and weaknesses are.

1. What is the basis for your faith in God?

2. How do you view Jesus Christ?

3. Do you remember at what age you began thinking about God as being someone much greater than you?

4. Did you talk about God and His Son, Jesus Christ, in your family?

5. How was the Christian faith explained to you?

6. How do you interpret your faith now?

7. Do you feel comfortable talking about your personal faith with your spouse? your child? a friend? your pastor?

8. When called on to tell your faith story, do you feel unsure of what to say?

23

9. Can you name five turning points in your life when God made Himself known to you?

10. Is prayer an important part of your Christian walk?

11. Have you experienced answers to prayers in the past week? Month? Year?

12. Do you have a specific prayer time each day? Do you keep a prayer list or calendar?

13. Do you have a specific time for Bible study each day?

14. Do you understand the Bible to be God's Holy Word?

15. Do you have a Bible prominently displayed in your home?

16. Do you read the Bible aloud to your children?

17. Can you recall any verses from memory?

18. Do you feel confident in the eternal life that Christians are promised?

19. Can you explain eternal life to your children when a loved one dies?

20. Have you talked with your children about God and your personal faith?

After you have completed the Faith Inventory, review your responses. Do you understand the Christian faith but hesitate in telling others the good news? Perhaps you are a student of the Bible but don't know how to interpret the verses to your children—on their level. Whatever the inventory reveals about your spiritual nature and personal faith walk, make plans today to strengthen your spiritual life and the spiritual foundation of your children.

PRACTICE SPIRITUAL STRENGTHS

Practice is important for developing spiritual strength. Think about it. What do you do in a workout? You run, climb stairs, swim, do aerobics, stretch, and more. You exercise to maintain or restore health. You do not exercise to gain a body, but to develop the one you already have.[6]

The good news is found in Ephesians 2:8–9, where Paul states that Christians are saved through faith. Acknowledging faith in Jesus Christ as Lord and Savior is the beginning of a personal relationship, a faith walk, with Him. Then spiritual growth takes time, just like physical growth.

Yet time is a precious commodity these days. Today's secular world offers many inventions that meet people's needs quickly and easily: instant foods, instant electronic communication, instant information stored in high-speed computers. Christians must remember, however, that there is no such thing as "instant maturity" in the Christian experience. Becoming a Christian begins a lifelong adventure of knowing God better and loving Him more.[7]

In Romans 12:2 we read: "Don't copy the behavior and customs of this world, but be a new and different person with a fresh newness in all you do and think. Then you will learn from your own experience how His ways will really satisfy you".

Remind yourself that to experience this faith walk—this transformation into God's man, God's woman, God's child—will take an ultimate act of trust. Yet the road to spiritual fulfillment will become a reality as you practice what the Bible teaches and encourage spiritual experiences for your children.

SPIRITUAL FOOD FOR THOUGHT

1. What kind of role model are you for your children when it comes to matters of the heart and spirituality? Do they see you praying or reading the Bible? Do they hear you tell of answered prayer, God's blessings, or miracles in your life?

2. Have you ever felt symptoms of "soul-sickness" as described on page 18? What caused these symptoms? When you are close to God in prayer, meditation, study, and fellowship, do you still have soul-sickness? Make an effort this week to stay in communion with Him, and see if it quiets your "inner circle."

3. Must you have control in everything you do? Write down ways that you like to be in control of life. Give God time each day this week to take control of your life. Write down your feelings as you do this.

4. Read the steps on pages 21 and 22 and renew your commitment to Jesus Christ. Pray daily that you will continue to follow His way as you strengthen your internal life.

5. Take the Faith Inventory and write down areas that you need to strengthen in your spiritual walk. Keep this list with your Bible and pray about each area this week, asking God for illumination.

Two

Tell Them the Stories of Jesus

"I know what God looks like," Brittnye announced smugly when she was in kindergarten. "He looks just like a beautiful little baby."

With that she pulled a picture of the baby Jesus out of her coloring book, remarking, "Jesus is God's Son, and Robbie is Daddy's son. Daddy looks like Robbie, so God looks like precious baby Jesus."

Children often make interesting analogies about God, Jesus, and their faith. They also ask profound questions about their faith and spirituality—many of which are difficult to answer. Their questions come from the active curiosity they have about all of life.

How do you answer their questions when you don't always know the answers? You give simple responses. After all, when God speaks, He doesn't always use big words! Yet before you begin doing this, take time to clarify your own views about your faith, and make a deliberate decision about which concepts you want to pass on to your child.

Remember that a child's concept of God as a loving Father is based on her relationship with you—her parent. If your relationship is full of love, acceptance, and affirmation, it will be easier for your child to understand that God also is a loving, accepting, affirming Father in heaven.

START YOUR CHILD'S FAITH WALK

Your child will start her faith walk as you put your own faith in Jesus Christ; this is the beginning of Christian growth. This maturing process thrives on spiritual nutrition, including

- prayer
- Bible study
- Christian fellowship
- listening to God

As you make a concerted effort to nurture your child's spiritual development, remember that true spirituality is not outward conformity to human rules and regulations or external adherence to a legalistic agenda. Nor is it not merely a subjective feeling or experience. True spirituality is inner renewal founded on and focused on Jesus Christ.[1] Developing spiritually means getting to know God through His Son.

What do you tell your child about Jesus Christ? About God the Father? To a child who views life in literal terms, abstract concepts can be confusing. Your child's age will determine her interpretation of God. According to author David Heller, four- to six-year-olds tend to see life in positive terms, viewing God as a simple, fun-loving entity. Children ages seven to nine may accept formal religious explanations of God's nature, yet harbor underlying questions, doubts, and fears. Children ages ten to twelve are the most inquisitive about God and the world, and the most likely to voice religious doubts. Preteens and teen-agers can understand Jesus as a personal friend, one who helps them with the trials of adolescence and comforts them in times of self-doubt and breaking away from family.

What's most basic to all life is the fact of life itself and how it begins, develops, and ends. For most of us, these are all deeply connected with our families. It has been said that family times are those moments when the course of life intersects with the power of love. But the map becomes most clear (and most challenging) in the person and life of Jesus. In Him, we find the intersection of life and love at its greatest intensity.[2]

Our hope is in the Word of the Lord. That's why the New Testament, which tells of Christ's ministry, is so important in our lives. A story is told of the brilliant writer, the late Katherine Mansfield, who came upon the Bible late in life, never having read or studied it until then. "I feel so bitterly," she wrote in her journal, "that I have never known these writings before. They ought to be part of my very breathing."

That is true of all of us! As parents of three children, we have opportunities each day to teach them about the love of Jesus Christ as taught in the Bible so that this knowledge becomes a part of their very breathing.

PARENTS CAN SHARE FAITH

Faith means commitment, trust, and caring for others. Faith enables us to risk sharing our lives with others in relationships. Because of faith that is nurtured in a loving Christian home, new lives are constantly being changed. Faith in a living Lord gives empty, lonely lives new meaning and purpose.

Faith also is an ongoing process. Theologians realize that just as people mature and grow in stages, so do we develop our faith, especially as our faith matures. Religious educators have found that just as a baby crawls before he walks and develops physically and mentally in sequence, so does our Christian faith.

In the book *Will Our Children Have Faith?*, author John Westerhoff III suggests four stages of faith development:

- *Experienced faith*—In this beginning stage, a person believes only what is experienced. Other people are observed and copied. This stage is highlighted by action and reaction towards others and events.

- *Affiliative faith*—The person moves into affiliating with significant people and events. Affiliative faith involves belonging, participation, and a feeling of being a part of something important.

- *Searching faith*—The person begins to use his mind to make critical judgments, including questioning and doubting, and to experiment with alternative courses of action.

- *Owned faith*—This is the ideal. Faith is truly "owned." The person begins to feel the need to tell others about her faith, to behave with an integrity that supports what she believes. [3]

We can encourage our children to grow in their faith by our example. Paul teaches in 1 Timothy 4:12: "Let no one despise your youth, but set the believers an example in speech and conduct, in love, in faith, in purity" (RSV). Example is so important for spiritual development, and parents have chances each day to model Christian living for their children. As we share our "owned faith" with our children, we must combine actions and words as we let the love of Christ move through us into their lives.

Our faith begins with an historical fact—the most important event in human history. The Christian faith asserts that nearly 2,000 years ago, God visited this tiny planet of ours in person. This is a statement outrageous enough to take our breath away. But it is the rock on which our faith is founded.

Jesus: More Than a Hero

We must emphasize with our children that Jesus is more than a hero of our faith. Heroes come and go. They have their day, then they are gone. That's not to say that heroes aren't important. Carlyle once said, "Society is founded on hero worship." Traditionally, many people, especially teen-agers, have modeled their lives after heroes. Yet Jesus is more than a hero of our faith. He *is* our faith. His life, death, and resurrection were the whole content of the early church's preaching. It is this content that we must teach our children as we proclaim that Jesus Christ was crucified, resurrected, and is triumphant forevermore.

As you talk with your children about Jesus, encourage them to learn the New Testament accounts with drama, role play, and dialogue:

- Read the account of Jesus' birth in the Gospel of Luke. Talk about how Joseph and Mary must have felt being the parents of the Christ child. Let younger children use robes and scarves to reenact the Nativity story.

- Tell about Jesus' boyhood. Share how He laughed, played, and even did household chores just like children today. Explain to your children that Jesus learned to crawl, walk, and talk just like they did.

- Share the story of Jesus in the temple during boyhood. We know that Jesus was brought up with religious teachings and that He was presented at the temple when he was just eight days old. Relate this experience to your child's baptism and talk about the importance of attending Sunday School and worship each week to learn more about God and His will for our lives.

- Discuss how Jesus learned just like children do today. Measure your child and talk about how the boy Jesus grew each day; relate this to your child's physical and spiritual growth.

- Emphasize how Jesus came to teach us how to live and love. He taught us what God is like. What examples of Christian love can your children give as they begin to understand the loving nature of Christ?

Talk about Your Belief in Christ

Many Christians believe that just "living" their faith in the home is their only duty as parents. As one young father told us, "I don't believe you have to talk about God in the home—to live my faith is enough." While being a role model and living your faith are vital to exemplify the selfless love of Jesus Christ, it's also important to talk about your personal faith with your children.

What can you say about God in your daily dialogue at home? You might say:

God has blessed us so much.
God has made you so special.
God has a wonderful plan for your life.
I thank God every day for you!
God will take care of you.

For some parents, just beginning a personal walk with the Lord, talking about their faith is difficult even with their children.

Yet there are easy ways to introduce God in your home. For example, you might say "God bless you" after a sneeze; "God is so good to us" after a family outing or holiday celebration; or "God loves you" when your child tells of a pleasant experience. When a young friend is sick, remind your child to pray for healing for her friend. When you serve a meal, let your child know that food comes from God's bountiful earth. When you pray as a family, join hands and tell your children how God gives strength to your family.

UNDERSTAND GOD THE FATHER

Parents can introduce children to a heavenly Father who cares about each one of His children. The Bible states that God is not only a Spirit and a Person, but a holy and righteous being. From Genesis to Revelation, God reveals Himself as a holy and perfect God. It is in God's holiness that we find the reason for the death of Christ. His holiness demanded the most exacting penalty for sin, and His love sent Jesus Christ to pay this penalty and provide man with salvation.[4]

Depending on their age and experiences, children view God in many different ways. A young child may see God as a "giver of gifts" similar to Santa Claus, while a teenager might tell of God being a personal friend and confidant. To all children, parents are the image of God. You can help your child interpret God as a warm and loving heavenly Father when you model this love in your home.

You can let your child see God as faithful when he knows he can count on you. Your child will see God's love as unconditional when you love your child for who he is—not what he does. He can see God as caring, compassionate, and nurturing when you provide for your child's needs and express your love for him through positive statements, hugs, and affirmation.

Questions Children Ask

Remember, when children ask questions about their faith, keep answers simple. The following questions and answers give an idea of how simplicity can enable a child to understand complicated topics without adding to their confusion.

What does God look like? Explain to your child that God is a spirit and doesn't have a body like human beings do. Jesus told us that "God is spirit, and those who worship him must worship in spirit and truth" (John 4:24, RSV). Spirits are invisible, so we can feel God's presence, but we do not see God as we see our parents or friends.

Who made God? It is important to tell your child that no one "made" God. He is the same yesterday, today, and forever. If someone "made" God, He would not be God; someone else would be more powerful! God is the Ultimate Being.

How do we know God is real? Although God does not look like us, people throughout history have experienced that nothing would exist without God's power and presence. Because He is a spirit, we do not see Him as an actual person or body, but we are touched by His works. God is everywhere, knows all things, and has no limits as humans do.

Does God ever leave us? Sometimes we feel God has abandoned us, especially when we are sad or hurt or when someone we love gets sick or dies. Yet we need to focus on the beauty in the world—the birds singing in the trees, the beautiful blue sky, the fragrant flowers, a precious baby—and know that God is here. We can feel the love of our moms and dads and know that God cares about us too.

Life in Christ Offers Hope to Teens

Just as the child is beginning to understand faith concepts, he hits adolescence. For many children, adolescent years bring conflicting emotions, thoughts, and behaviors. As your teen continues his faith walk in Christ's church, you can feel assured that his spiritual foundation is taking hold—though it may not seem like it at times. When our son Rob was a sophomore in college, he called one night to thank us for introducing him to Jesus when he was a child. Was this the same child who complained of being too tired to get up on Sunday mornings during teenage years at home? Rob told us he knew that his Christian faith enabled him to cope with the adversities of college life—and wanted to share this with the young men in his dormitory.

What do church youths think about God? Researchers at the Search Institute asked this question to 2,365 Protestant seventh to twelfth graders. Here are their responses:

- God is loving—97 percent

- God accepts me the way I am—95 percent

- God is active in individuals—79 percent

- God is a close friend—78 percent

- God is working for social change—73 percent

- God has a plan for my life—56 percent[5]

JESUS, THE SON

The chart on page 37 shows what we know to be true: Our children and teenagers want and need a loving heavenly Father in their lives. Yet no one comes to the Father except by the Son, and we can encourage our children to develop a personal relationship with Jesus Christ.

What does a personal relationship with Jesus Christ mean?

- It means letting Jesus make a difference in your life.

- It means finding in Christ the foremost clues about God's nature, His work, and His will.

- It means allowing ourselves to be changed and transformed by God's love.

- It means changing our self-centered, selfish living and letting God's higher purposes take over our lives.

- It means trying to think, live, and act like Christ would, regardless of whether we feel like it.

Remind your child that a personal relationship with Jesus Christ is not a feeling. If that were the case, some of the strongest Christians would totally give up on days they didn't feel like "loving" others.

Jesus Was Both Human and Divine

As your child reaches elementary-school age, he will begin to understand the often-confusing concept that, while Jesus was fully human, He was also fully divine.

Your child needs to understand the ultimate effort of God to convey His love to us in Jesus Christ. The entire New Testament witnesses to that. Jesus lived and died His love for us. He also used the simplest human images to give flesh to His love. He chose, for example, the image of a shepherd, so familiar to His hearers. They knew the devotion of a shepherd for his sheep. So, Jesus dared to say, "I am the good shepherd; I know my own, and my own know me . . . and I lay down my life for the sheep" (John 10:14–15, RSV).[6] God did not choose to come to earth as a rich ruler or a powerful king. He came simply and humbly as a baby born to loving parents.

What If?

Talk with your older child and teen about how our lives would be different today if Jesus had not come. If Jesus had not come:

- We would not enjoy all the blessings we have from our relationship with Him.

- We would not experience the joy and peace with God that He made possible through His life, death, and resurrection.

- We would not know God in the intimate, personal way that Jesus revealed Him to us.

- We would not send missionaries to the far corners of the world to share the good news of Christ with others.

- We would not have great churches in this country and around the world.

- We would not have the great teaching institutions of our denominations to train preachers and teachers in God's Word.

- We would not have the New Testament as a part of Scripture—the Golden Rule, the Sermon on the Mount.

- We would not have the magnificent hymns that are so much a part of our Christian heritage.

- We would not understand the self-less, *agape* love that Christ lived and taught.[7]

Jesus Died for Our Sins

Talking about Jesus with children would not be complete without emphasizing that Jesus loved us so much that He died for the sins of all humankind, rose from the dead, and lives eternally. Tell your child that Jesus was buried, much like our friends and family members are buried, and just as we will be buried someday. When the great stone was finally sealed to the opening of Jesus' tomb, His loved ones experienced the finality of His life. Yet this grief-stricken vigil at the grave on Good Friday changed into the joy of Easter morning, for Scripture tells us that on the third day after Jesus' death, He rose again. He is alive!

A story we have shared with our teenagers concerns John Quincy Adams when he was eighty. A friend met him on the street and asked how he was that day. Adams brightly replied, "John Quincy Adams is very well, thank you. But the house in which he lives is becoming dilapidated; it is tottering on its foundation. I think John Quincy Adams will have to move out of it before very long. But he, himself, is very well, thank you."[8]

Knowing that who we really are—our spirit—will live forever is a vital part of being a Christian, and faith is something on which our entire being depends.

The celebration of the Christian faith is that no matter what obstacles our physical body faces on earth, we know that someday our spirit will have life eternal with our heavenly Father. Paul tells us that because Jesus was raised from the dead, we are raised too. Christians know that the grave does not have the final say in our life, because we believe the grave did not have the final say in Christ's life.

THE HOLY SPIRIT GUIDES US

The Holy Spirit is God's special gift to those who believe in His Son, Jesus Christ. This Spirit of God lives within each Christian. As we learn more about our faith through Bible study, prayer, and worship, and grow closer to our heavenly Father, we will recognize this Holy Spirit within us.

Jesus taught us, "And I will pray [to] the Father, and he will give you another Counselor, to be with you forever, even the Spirit of truth, whom the world cannot receive, because it neither sees him nor knows him; you know him, for he dwells with you, and will be in you" (John 14:16–17, RSV).

Teaching that God is present every day in our lives is important for parents as you talk about the Holy Spirit. Let your child know that this Spirit is not like a ghost and is nothing to be frightened about, but is the Spirit of God who will offer guidance, protection, and strength to those who acknowledge Him.

What Is the Trinity?

The Trinity encompasses God the Father, God the Son, and God the Holy Spirit. You can explain the Trinity to your child by telling him that God is our heavenly Father, Jesus is God's Son, and the Holy Spirit is a daily friend and helper who is with us always.

In her book *Helping Your Teen Develop Faith,* Delia Touchton Halverson admits the Trinity is a difficult theological concept, even for adults, but crucial. "We worship one God, yet the one God is shown in three ways: God the creator, God in human form, and God within us," she writes. "Jesus was the God in human form. Because God came as Jesus, in human form, we are able to realize that God knows what it is like to be human. Through Christ, God experienced human temptations, human rejection and loneliness, human stress and frustration, human sorrow and pain. Because he suffered, we can have a closer relationship to God. We know that God has lived the experience with which we are struggling and knows that experience as a human."[9]

SEEK ASSISTANCE

Because children's spiritual development is an important part of their overall growth, parents often need assistance in guiding them. You can seek information on spirituality and the Christian faith from your pastor, Christian friends, your church library, Christian bookstores or Christian magazines, such as *Living with Teenagers, ParentLife, Home Life, Christian Parenting Today,* and *Parents of Teenagers.*

Share Your Faith

As your child gets older you can begin to share your personal faith in how God, through Jesus Christ, has touched your life. We know the impact it had when people shared their faith with us. Now the challenge is ours to continue the 2,000-year legacy of the Christian faith by sharing with our children.

You can talk with your toddler or preschooler about God as his heavenly Father as you tell about the works of God. You can point to a colorful rainbow, a brilliant sunset, or a soft baby as examples of God's love for all people. Relationships such as these establish a link in a child's mind between God and nature, God and loved ones, God and beauty.

As children reach elementary school age, many parents ask, "What exactly do I say when I find that perfect time to share my faith?" You simply tell your child what you believe and what you have personally experienced. This is the best way to explain the gospel. You don't have to "preach" or memorize passages from the Bible; you relate your Christian experience to your child by genuinely sharing what you have experienced.

Bob tells of sharing his faith story this way with Rob when he was eight years old:

> When I was fifteen, I really wondered if there was a God. I felt so empty and lonely. My mother had recently died, and I was confused. One night I was sitting outside by myself watching the sunset over the Gulf of Mexico. Looking at the majestic sunset, I was so overcome with this power, this perfect love, that I knew could only be of God. I spoke with my pastor, and he helped me to invite Jesus Christ to come into my life. Then I became active in a teen

Bible study and Sunday School so I could learn more about God. Although I questioned my faith in early college years, by the time I was a senior in college I knew that God had called me into the ministry. I feel that my questioning period made my faith walk even stronger.

What is your faith story? Do you remember the time you asked Jesus Christ into your life, or did you grow up knowing the Lord's love? How has God helped you through trials in life? Try to make your faith story come from the "eyes of your soul." Use this sharing time as a way to get personal with your child and with God so your child will want to seek the same fulfillment and blessings you have experienced.

Jesus' final commandment is to us, as recorded in Matthew 28, "Go into all the world and make disciples . . . and teach." That commandment begins with our personal witness at home as we share our faith with our children and pray for a "gracious confrontation," providing that home environment where God's grace can be experienced and an "owned" faith in our Lord Jesus Christ can result.

Share God's Grace

As you share your faith, let your child feel comfortable in expressing emotions, concerns, personal joys, and frustrations without fear of being teased or ridiculed. You can provide such a secure atmosphere in your home that feelings can be expressed by you leading the way. During intimate times of faith sharing, interject your personal history. Tell of struggles you had as a child, teen, and adult. Tell how God helped you cope with crises or disappointments.

Describe how you felt in the situation. Talk about your emotions in terms your child can understand—the pounding heart that accompanies being afraid or nervous, the pain in the stomach that goes with loneliness, the dull feeling that accompanies depression.

As you risk being open and talking about your life struggles as a Christian, your child will begin to feel comfortable enough to express his feelings within the safety of your home.

WHAT ABOUT DOUBTING THOMAS?

When Michael, our nephew, was seven years old, Deb's sister took him aside. She quietly shared that, even though he would be disappointed, it was time for him to know that Santa Claus was not real. Young Michael took this reality exceptionally hard, crying out, "Santa Claus is not real? The next thing you'll tell me is that the Easter Bunny and Jesus aren't real, too!"

We expect children to trust us unquestioningly; yet in the early years of their lives, we earnestly tell them myths and even lies. For example, how many of us have mysteriously said, "No, that wasn't Daddy. It was one of Santa's helpers"? Or "Now go find all the eggs the Easter Bunny left in the yard." On a more serious note, many of us have explained death to a young child by saying, "Grandma's just sleeping. She will be asleep for a very long time."

If you think sharing Jesus Christ with your child is difficult now, you may face an even greater stumbling block as she matures and begins to doubt the existence of God, especially during the teen years.

"Why should I believe in God?" Fourteen-year-old Ben asked us when his younger brother was diagnosed with terminal cancer. "If God is love, He would never allow something like this to happen." Julie, a sixteen-year-old teen, refused to attend church as she told us that all Christians were "hypocrites." And seventeen-year-old Matt spent his senior year debating his Sunday school teacher about the existence of God.

Adolescence is a time for breaking away as teens establish their independence. Spiritual questioning is just one of the many ways they separate from parents. During these rebellious and questioning years, teens are often filled with doubts about a personal faith in God. By this age, many young people have experienced the sadness of having a loved one die. They have felt the rejection of failure—by losing in sports, not winning a class election, failing a test in school. Teens have felt unloved when peers mock or snub them, siblings team up against them, and parents misunderstand their problems. Many have experienced what they may consider to be unanswered prayers when the world comes crashing in as parents argue, or even divorce.

"If there is a God, He sure isn't looking after me," fifteen-year-old Erin said angrily after her father lost his job and the family had to relocate to another town to find employment.

How can parents help during this questioning period? We must remain open and genuine with our own faith, and let our child know we have struggles and doubts of our own from time to time. Becoming a "perfect" example is one goal we humans cannot reach. As Christian parents, we don't have to know all the answers. In fact, we can relieve ourselves of much guilt as we tell our teens of doubts we've had and how we struggle to resolve them, referring them through Bible study and prayer.

You also can help teens overcome doubt by explaining that there are at least two ways to think about life. For example, when your teen works long and hard on a tough math problem, she might finally say, "I got it!" Another way is when your teen goes to a great movie and it changes her. In that case it gets her![10]

So it is with God's grace. The intangible nature of faith and the existence of God can be addressed through experience, assurance, and the presence of the Spirit. It gets us; rarely do we grab it. To reconcile doubts, it's helpful to look backward. When your teen looks back several years, he will vividly see God's hand in his life—guiding, protecting, comforting, and sustaining.

Let your child know that having doubts is not wrong, but allowing doubts to control him and his behavior is. You can model a living example of God's love as your child sees you in action in the home and at work. Teens need to see examples of the "God (who) is at work in you, both to will and to work for his good pleasure" (Phil. 2:13, RSV).

When your teen expresses doubts about faith, teach him to seek answers for the doubts with worship attendance, Bible study, and prayer. Encourage him to get involved in Christian youth programs where other teens can share their struggles and receive guidance from mature believers.

THE BIBLE TEACHES US ABOUT JESUS

As you introduce Jesus to your child, teach her that we get to know Him in different ways—through prayer, through others, through studying God's Word. The Bible is central to our understanding of the Christian faith; it teaches us God's plan for our lives as we see God's love in action. In 2 Timothy 3:16–17, we find that the Bible is God's way of making us well prepared at every point, "equipped for every good work" (RSV). The Bible is divinely inspired by God and teaches us what is true and false—right and wrong. While reading the Bible for inspiration is important for Christians, careful Bible study is necessary as we learn how to apply Scriptures to our daily lives.

Older children and teens can understand that the Bible is the most remarkable Book ever written. It was brought to us by about forty men of many occupations. They wrote over a period of approximately 1,500 years, and in three languages—Hebrew, Aramaic, and Greek. The Bible consists of sixty-six books and is divided into two parts, the Old Testament and the New Testament (the word *testament* means covenant). Yet, for all its variety, the Bible has one great theme and central figure: Jesus Christ. That would be impossible unless the Bible had one supreme author: the Holy Spirit of God.[11]

The word *inspiration* comes from a Greek word meaning "*God-breathed.*" This concept will confuse young children as they wonder if God really did "breathe" into Bible writers. You can explain

"God-breathed" as "that which was written by men was breathed out by God." God spoke to the writers of His Word; they were His spokesmen.[12]

Share the Bible with Your Child

Have you ever read the Scriptures to your children at bedtime, only to realize you need more practical examples to relate the biblical message to their young minds? Perhaps you have drawn a blank in interpreting the Scriptures in a personal way?

Teaching our children the stories in the Bible and referring to scriptural examples are two of the oldest tools for communicating our Christian faith. Our Lord told parables to crowds of people as He taught of God's love. These parables—or stories with a message—helped to explain the Scriptures in terms the people could understand.

In our families, we learn of our heritage and traditions by listening to personal stories handed down through the generations. The favorite phrase at bedtime in many homes is often, "Please, just one more story."

Using real-life stories and personal anecdotes can enhance your biblical teaching in the family. These examples can make the Scriptures clearer, more relevant to today's life, and convincing to your children.

Yet telling stories and sharing personal experiences at home is not as easy as it may seem. Perhaps the following suggestions could help you bring the Bible to life as you enhance and relate the message of the gospels to vivid stories.

Make it true. Stories that aren't true aren't as convincing, especially to discerning teens. Somehow, human nature can tell fact from fable. How can you find good examples to explain Scriptures? Let's look at two key ways:

1. *Get personal.* The most convincing examples are those you have experienced. Begin by keeping a personal journal or

encounter book. Each day, jot down experiences or insights that have revealed God to you. Write down your questions, doubts, fears, as well as your answers to prayer and spiritual awakenings. Then, as you read the Bible to your children, reflect on this journal and find situations that might relate to the Scripture's emphasis. You don't have to be the hero or heroine of the story! Perhaps God became real to you through your mistake or failure. Don't tell the story with the intention of glorifying yourself. Rather, look for anecdotes that help to glorify God.

2. *Collect examples.* Listen to people around you—at home, at church, and at work. Write down interesting experiences you may hear of how God became real in the lives of others. Avoid using anecdotes or stories that would embarrass anyone, and change names of real people as appropriate.

Another excellent resource for finding stories to tell your children is Christian magazines, books, and your local newspaper. Clip out relevant information and articles or jot down the particulars, and keep them tucked away in your journal.

Make it Specific. If you say, "Many people have used prayer in their lives with miraculous results," you've hardly convinced your children. Try this: "Here's a magazine article where the author tells of his struggle with prayer. Listen to the miraculous answers he experienced." Even the most rebellious teenager or distracted child may tune in to the message you are trying to teach. Your believability increases as you describe particular incidents in detail.

Make the story active. You don't have to memorize a story or example word for word, but you'll be more effective if you study the message of the account. Have a clear understanding of the characters involved—their names, their personalities, their relationship with one another. It is also vital to understand the plot and how the various segments of the story fit together. If you become uncertain of how to relate an anecdote or story to your children, read straight from the article or book where you found it.

Make it relate to scriptures. Ask yourself, How does this story relate to the verses I'm reading to my children? Consciously sort through your life, your journal, and your collection of examples to find the specific anecdotes that can enhance the verses you read and your personal goals.

Make the story an experience. Children become even more involved in a story if you allow them to experience it in a variety of ways. The story may be written on cards and used as a role play or mini-drama for the children to act out. As they take on the various roles of the characters, they can interpret the story as one with meaning in their own lives. You may prepare questions to ask your children regarding the meaning of the role play after they finish. Talk with your children about the story they act out so the meaning is experienced.

Costumes can be worn by you or your children to give more life to the story being told. Props can be added to give even more credence to the story. For example, if it's about a woman who encountered God while traveling alone one night, you might use a prop like an overnight case to add interest to the story. This will allow your children to "feel" more what the character in the story was truly feeling.

Use tools to assist you. If you find that you can't tell stories to your children without losing your train of thought, you can always record the stories and play the tape to them. You may have friends or family members record the voices on the tapes, use background music for added emphasis, and fill in when necessary with the narration of the story—giving location, time, place, and other important specifics. The added benefit of taped stories is that children can listen to them when you're away.[13]

FAMILY TIME

Helping your child to understand the Bible and its importance to her life is a daily task. Challenge your child or teen to learn the following Bible facts, then check off the list as they share them with you:

- The difference between the Old and New Testaments
- The books of the Old Testament
- The Ten Commandments
- The books of the New Testament
- The Four Gospels
- The Lord's Prayer (Matt. 6:9–13)
- The names of the twelve disciples
- Psalm 23
- John 3:16
- The Beatitudes

SPIRITUAL FOOD FOR THOUGHT

1. How are you responding to your personal Savior in your home? Is your relationship with Jesus Christ making a difference in your attitude toward others? In your tolerance level of your children? In your outlook on life? In your priorities? In your involvement in the church? In your personal witness?

2. What areas do you need to work on to live the *agape* love that Jesus taught? What would it take to make these changes? Write down three positive steps you will take this week to make these changes, and keep this list with you during the week. Refer to it when your behavior falls back into old habits, but don't condemn yourself for failing to meet your expectations. Remember, God is patient with us, as we should be with others.

3. One of the greatest witnesses you can have is to share the love of our Lord with someone who is in despair. Watch for

signs in your family this week of a child or spouse who is feeling out-of-sorts or without hope. Be a witness for our Lord and share His love and assurance. Did this witness change you? The other person?

4. It is so easy to love the child who doesn't challenge the way of our Lord in the home, but what about the strong-willed or defiant child? Is there a child in your family who needs to be "loved" into a personal relationship with Jesus Christ? Put this child at the top of your prayer list and work at loving him even when he is "unlovable."

5. Begin a spiritual journal and write down answers to prayer and situations where you feel God is in control.

Three

Understand the
Role of Christ's Church

When Brittnye was six years old, she became distraught when her eight-year-old brother told her he was going to buy a butterfly net to use the next weekend to catch butterflies and put them in jars for his collection. For several nights as we tucked her into bed, Brittnye earnestly prayed, "Please, dear Jesus, let Rob's new net get holes in it so he won't hurt my beautiful butterflies."

We were impressed at the strength of Brittnye's childlike faith. On Saturday morning, while we were eating breakfast, she came into the kitchen beaming, telling us that Jesus had finally answered her prayers. "My butterflies are going to be fine!" she declared.

"Brittnye, why do you think your prayer will be answered today?" we asked, surprised at her confidence in God's intervention.

She smiled knowingly and replied, "Because last night I took my school scissors and cut holes in the net!"

Perhaps this is a silly childhood memory, but it sure illustrates the point that prayer and works go hand in hand! We all must pray and work for the good things Christ taught, lived, and died for. As we make a commitment to be faithful to Christ's church, we promise to pray for the church, for ourselves, and for others. Yet along with this ongoing prayer go works and commitment.

WE ARE THE CHURCH

You are the church. I am the church. We are the church together. Most of us describe our church by the outward appearance of its physical plant, such as "the red brick church with the tall steeple." Yet the church is not the building at all; it is the people. And it is through these people—brothers and sisters in Christ Jesus—that you and your child will receive faith affirmation.

The church is the family of God bound together in God's abundant love through Jesus Christ. As a united family in Christ, the church strives to worship God, to love Him, and to join together in ministry to others as it teaches the gospel message. At its best, the church is on mission to all God's people as it ministers with acceptance, love, and forgiveness.

As you become spiritual soulmates with your child, the church will play an important part in reinforcing your disciplines at home, for the church is about experiencing the fullness of the Christian life. Our commitment to Jesus Christ is a life decision—the most important decision any of us will ever make.

Worshiping in Christ's church each week allows us to have new beginnings in life. We come to hear the Word read and preached, to sing the great hymns of the faith, to confess our sins, to make our petitions, and to offer our praise. Worship provides an environment for God's grace to be encountered and for decisions to be made to follow Him.

When Jacob encountered God at Bethel, he cried out, "Surely the LORD is in the place; and I did not know it. . . . How awesome is this place! This is none other than the house of God, and this is the gate of heaven" (Gen. 28:16–17, RSV). Every time we enter into our church, we must be prepared, like Jacob, to encounter God.

Knowing Christ opens up a whole new dimension to church membership. The creeds, liturgies, prayers, and anthems that seemed so routine and lifeless before now shine with grace. Hymns that once only filled time before the sermon sound sweeter as their message comes alive in our hearts. A transformation takes place.

TRANSFORMATION STARTS WITH COMMITMENT

A Commitment to Christ

Being a Christian and belonging to a local church go hand and hand. Our first commitment is to Christ. When we join Christ's church, the first promise we make is a commitment to Jesus Christ as our Lord and Savior. We ask Jesus to live in our heart and we allow His Spirit to make a difference in the way that we live and relate to others. When we say Jesus is our "Lord," we mean that He controls our entire life; Jesus is the model by which we live. When we say Jesus is our "Savior," we mean that He saves us "from" some things and "for" other things. Jesus saves us from *selfishness* and enables us to *selflessness.* We express God's love for us by giving ourselves. Jesus also saves us "for" service in His name and we become sensitive to the concerns and the needs of others.

A Commitment to Receive the Faith

Our second commitment is to receive the Christian faith as taught in the Scriptures. The Bible is our Book, and without it we would not be the church. The Old Testament tells us about our past heritage, and the New Testament teaches us about Christ and the church. Understanding the Scriptures, like being a Christian, is a life-long process, and we must always strive to learn more. For many of us, this one hour of worship each week is a time when we shift our burden from our shoulders to God's. We find strength in the Word of the Lord, and that is why the Scriptures are so important to us.

A Commitment to Be Faithful and Pray

When we join the church, we promise to be faithful to Christ through this church and to live that commitment with our prayers, our presence, our gifts, and our service. This commitment goes beyond once-a-week church attendance; it means living our faith every day of our lives—whether we feel like it or not.

A Commitment of Presence

Our presence also is important to this commitment of church membership. We promise to be faithful in our attendance. For parents, this means actively involving ourselves in the life of the church—Sunday School, Bible studies, music programs, men's and women's groups, worship, and more. Many parents feel their duty stops with taking their children to church, but we believe parents must model commitment by attending classes, leading groups, and celebrating worship together—as a family.

For parents who seek to nurture spirituality in their children, the church provides training in the Christian faith. The church offers a sense of belonging to members of all ages as they tell others with pride: "That's my church!" For children to continue worshiping in the church as adults, it is important that they have strong family involvement during childhood.

Why Worship as a Family	
When Mom and Dad both attend regularly:	72 percent of their children remain faithful later in life.
When only Dad attends:	55 percent remain faithful.
When only Mom attends:	15 percent remain faithful.
When neither parent attends:	6 percent remain faithful.

A Commitment to Give

Commitment to Christ's church means promising to be faithful with our gifts. The Bible teaches us to tithe, which means giving 10 percent of our earnings to God. Jesus said more about what we do with our money than about any other subject. He taught that what we do with our money indicates what kind of person we are and where our real commitments lie. Christ calls us to make a real offering of our whole self to Him—our talents, our time, our abilities, and our money.

A Commitment to Service

When we join a church, we also make a commitment to serve. This service can be given inside or outside of the church. God's work can be carried on at school, on the job, in leisure time, and in community activities as well as within the church. Service means giving of yourself. It's making your whole life reflect Christ's Spirit living in you.

Joining a church means commitment—a commitment of prayers, presence, gifts, and service. To some people who have never made this commitment to Christ's church, it can seem overwhelming. We have always taught our three children to "believe that you can!" Every time they use the word *can't,* we always say, "You *can,* you just won't." That is an important lesson in life, especially in being a disciple of Christ. You must believe that you can. Whoever you are, whatever your failures may be, no matter how difficult and dark your future may appear, you still *can* become a disciple of Christ and be obedient to Him with a commitment to Christ's church.

Jesus Christ looked into the faces of one of the motliest crews of ordinary men and women ever assembled and told them they could change the world. They believed Him and set about doing it—with His Spirit. Joining a church and really making a commitment to serve Him means being a part of a fellowship of believers where God's love reigns.

A COMMUNITY OF BELIEVERS

Belonging to a church and attending as a family helps children realize they belong to a larger community. And that sense of belonging is pivotal. Being part of a spiritual community implies not only feeling cared for, but also caring for others.

The search for spirituality addresses the issue of loneliness, which is very real for many people today. It gives shape to the search for meaning in life. It encourages people to reach out to one another.[1]

When Christians work together and reach out to others, the impossible becomes possible. Churches around the world have united to accomplish great feats of caring for the poor. Mission fields in our country and across the globe are alive with Christian men and women who receive training and support from local churches. Churches join with others in their community to host spiritual emphasis services, revivals, or Christian concerts—all while bringing the message of Jesus Christ to the unsaved.

"BUT I DON'T WANT TO GO"

One of the most common questions parents ask is, "Should I make my child go to church if he doesn't want to?" In our own home, Rob, Brittnye, and Ashley all went through the developmental "breaking away" phases. Each expressed a temporary loss of interest in the church and youth activities. Still, we firmly believe that church attendance is not a choice for children: it is an act of faith that our family believes in—whether all members are interested at that moment or not.

What about a teen's involvement with the local church, especially as he seeks to distance himself from parental involvement and to establish his own identity? Many studies have shown that teens who identify with and commit to a purpose greater than themselves find life meaningful and challenging. As most of us have experienced, nonreligious causes ultimately will come up short. Only a purpose that comes from God resists the trials of life and storms of adolescence to offer ultimate meaning and purpose. The local church can serve this purpose.

Parents Are Called to Prepare the Way

For many parents, one of the most difficult tasks is encouraging teens to commit themselves fully to the church, accepting the responsibilities and privileges that accompany membership or confirmation. At this often-rebellious stage, perhaps the most important thing parents can do is to personally model active involvement in the local congregation.

In essence, being a Christian and belonging to a church go hand in hand. When we join a church, we promise to be faithful to Christ through this church, and to live that commitment with our prayers, our presence, our gifts, and our service. This commitment goes far beyond once-a-week church attendance. It means living our faith every day of our lives—whether we feel like it or not. It is this ongoing, daily commitment that must be shared with our teens.

How many adults would rather sleep in on a rainy day or miss church because we were out too late the night before? But our children model our behavior. If we make a regular effort to get up, get dressed, and get to church each week—because it is a priority in our lives—our children and teens will do the same. Encouraging them to make a regular commitment—even when they don't feel like it—will help them see that they belong to a much larger community—the body of Christ within the local church.

Being part of a spiritual community means not only feeling cared for, but also caring for others. When we join a church or are confirmed, we make a commitment to service, which can be given in the church, at school, in our families, on the athletic field, and in community activities as we live our Christian discipleship.

Service to others involves making our lifestyle reflect Christ's Spirit living in us. Two examples of service through the local church are when teens assist with Vacation Bible School or serve as greeters at worship. Not only are these acts of benevolence and giving rewarding for teens needing confidence and acceptance, but they also place the teens into a new realm of discipleship as they learn to put "feet to faith."

Church membership can help teens form their personal identity as they participate in worship, youth programs, committees, choirs, and mission outreach. Leadership commitment also affords teens a way to use their God-given talents and gifts as they sing in church, perform a skit for shut-ins, or feed the homeless.

As we encourage our teens to fully immerse themselves in the life of the church, they will move into the development of a personal faith based on reflective thinking. Through Bible study, teens will gain a new understanding of human behavior and find answers for their many questions regarding religious faith. They also can grow from relationships with other adults in the church, not just parents.

The Challenge of the Church

Are we truly challenging young people to be fully connected to the local church? In a study demonstrating what teenagers were interested in learning from their church, the following represents some possible starting places:

- 74 percent want to learn friendship-making skills.

- 71 percent want to learn to know and love Jesus Christ.

- 69 percent want to learn more about who God is.

- 68 percent want to learn to make decisions about right and wrong.

- 65 percent want to gain a sense of purpose in life.

- 61 percent want to develop more compassion and concern for people.

(Source: Search Institute 1989 survey of 2,365 Protestant youths.)

Choosing a Church

Evangelist Billy Graham has said that, "Each Christian should select his church because he is convinced that within its particular structure he will find the greatest opportunities for spiritual growth, the greatest satisfactions for his human needs, and the greatest chance to be of helpful service to those around him."[3]

If you don't have a church home for your family, the following questions can give guidance as you select a congregation that meets your family's special needs and seek opportunities for involvement where Christ is intentionally offered and lives are changed.

What does this church believe? Is it committed to teaching the Bible? Your church is your spiritual home. Worship services and study groups can help you meet the challenges of living in a secular society as a Christian, or they can leave you with a feeling of emptiness. The church you join should help you receive and feel the power of God's love through Bible-based teaching. Discussion and study groups should help you and family members understand God's Word and Christ's teachings so they relate to your life today.

What programs does this church offer for my family and my children? To meet the needs of all members of your family, your church should have ongoing programs for everyone, from toddlers and teens to senior adults. The church is the one organization in our society where men and women of all ages join together in a common fellowship. Make sure your church offers support and inspiration to all your family members.

Are children and teens encouraged to participate fully in the life of the church? Along with special age-appropriate programs, children and teens need to feel as if they belong to their church—not just to its Sunday School or youth group. Teens can serve on committees in many churches and stand up for issues that relate to youth today. Children can participate in many activities, including mission projects.

Do programs focus on family issues? What about the family dinners, retreats, or seminars offered at your church? Do they help families grow in faith? Family-friendly churches should have an ongoing mission to the families in their congregation and community with parenting seminars, speakers on family issues, musical programs geared for children and teens, and more. "Family is important here" should be a clear message of your congregation.

Are there opportunities for me to serve here? Some people enjoy the excitement of helping to start a church, while others feel more at home with a traditional, established church. If you have time and energy and are willing to work hard at discipleship and evangelism, maybe God is leading you to help get a new church off the ground. We have never seen a church turn away a willing volunteer. Where there are willing hands, there will be a need.

Don't wait to be "invited" to participate in the life of your church. Most busy pastors face too many daily demands to personally invite each member to teach, share, or lead in the church. Consider this your motivation to go beyond yourself and find your "niche" in the church, using your God-given talents and abilities to glorify His name.

Would I feel comfortable inviting my friends to come here? Surprising as it seems, many people do not feel comfortable inviting their friends to church. If you feel hesitant in doing so, think of the reasons why, then take steps to change these stumbling blocks into steppingstones for Christ. One friend shared that she hadn't invited anyone to attend her church because the members stuck to themselves after worship, rarely inviting newcomers to join their groups. "After I shared this concern with the board members of the church, we had a campaign to become an 'inviting' church, and the results were astounding," she reported. "People who had not welcomed guests in years were going out of their way to greet people. It's just what we needed—a wake-up call for discipleship."

Does the church encourage intergenerational activities? They say that youths give enthusiasm to the elderly; the elderly give wisdom to youths. Churches can provide opportunities for all members to participate in fellowship and learning experiences through intergenerational assemblies, family night suppers, study groups, volunteer projects, and more.

CAN YOUNG CHILDREN WORSHIP TOO?

Worship is a celebration for Christians. The quietness of the sanctuary, the soothing chords from the organ, and the choir's majestic anthem all add to a worshipful experience. Yet often, when we include young children in the services, our meditative thoughts are abruptly interrupted by a small child tugging at our sleeve, saying, "Is it almost over yet?" or, "Can I go to the bathroom . . . again?"

Worship is communion with God. It is also our response to God's love, and this response is a vital part of the Christian family's spiritual commitment. Our children begin to develop their own faith as they join us in worshiping God with liturgies, songs, and prayers.

In Proverbs 22:6, we learn to "Train children in the right way, and when old, they will not stray" (NRSV). How can you train your young child to experience meaningful worship?

Practice whispering. Do this in the car on the way to church and as you walk to Sunday School class. Let your child know that we whisper during worship so we don't disturb the pastor, the choir, and those around us. Quiet voices show respect to God and others.

Go to the sanctuary before the service, when it's empty and quiet. Tell your child that this is a special place to think and learn about God and Jesus. Explain the different parts to your child—the altar, the baptismal font, the pulpit, the lectern, the pews, and communion rail. Use your "whisper" voice inside the sanctuary, and encourage your child to practice doing the same.

Before worship, point out the different symbols in your church and give a simple explanation of their meaning. While some may not have meaning to your child, he can understand a cross and will associate Jesus with this Christian symbol.

Explain to your child that worship is where we praise and thank God. Smile frequently at your child throughout the service, let him lean on you when he gets tired, and hold his hand during the prayer. Make his experience a positive one as you share God's love.

Bring a pack of crayons to church with you and help your child mark a line on the bulletin as each part of the service is completed. This will give her an idea of when the service is coming to a close. Encourage your church to provide special children's activity bulletins available through most denominational publishing houses.

Be prepared for your child to become restless during the service. Bring blank paper for your child to draw, and a small bag of cereal will keep even the most active child busy and quiet.

Sing some favorite hymns at home and let your child listen to these on tape. This will help to familiarize her with the music used on Sunday morning. Two tapes of children's hymns include "My First Hymns" and "Wee Sing Bible Songs" (Word).

Include the child in adult worship. Let him help you hold the hymnal and the Bible. Bring his children's picture Bible to worship and look up the Scriptures in this version.

When the offering plate is passed, make sure your child has coins to drop into the plate. With your help, let him pass it to the next person. Talk about how the money goes to help needy children or other ministries.

Let your child greet the pastor each week after services, and make sure the pastor knows her name. This will give the child added impetus to pay attention, knowing that she is important to her pastor.

If your child has difficulty sitting still, choose a more informal service, such as the early service or a Saturday evening service. Many parents find that sitting in the balcony of the church also helps to keep the child's interest.

Don't make worship a negative experience—for you or your child. If your child cannot sit through the entire service without getting fussy or kicking the pew in front of him, let him stay for the hymns and prayers, then escort him to the nursery or children's church for the remainder of the time.

THE ROLE OF THE CHURCH

The ultimate worth of a child is in the hands and hearts of each of us. We can ignore the needs of the precious children around us, or we can surround them with unconditional Christ-like love, nurture, and acceptance. If children are to grow into a personal relationship with Jesus Christ and become the people God intended, we must take seriously our duty to provide protection, education, and stability.

Spirituality must be nurtured in the home each day in order for it to develop in the child. Yet what about children whose parents do not care or who don't come from a Christian home? The church must place all children in highest esteem through innovative age-level programs that meet the needs of these younger Christians. Churches can organize:

- creative Sunday School classes

- children's Bible stories and participation during worship

- midweek enrichment programs

- after-school programs for "latchkey" children

- visitation in the homes of new parents, inviting them to the church

- safe and clean nurseries for the very young and vulnerable

- active children's and youth choirs that teach of God's love

- ongoing transportation for children and youths when parents are unable to bring them to church

Local Mission

Our neighborhoods and cities are filled with children who are hurt daily by physical, sexual, and emotional abuse at the hands of the very adults they look up to and trust. Christians are called to minister to these children directly, support benevolent giving through the church, make generous donations to local child-support agencies, and stay abreast of political initiatives that can help rescue these abused children.

Global Mission

As we focus on the value of children in our lives, the responsibility of Christians doesn't stop at our city limits or national borders. Across the globe are millions of children who go to bed each night without food to nourish their starving bodies. These same children also hunger and thirst for spiritual nourishment—words of comfort, assurance, and strength that only the love of Jesus Christ can give. Christians in the church can touch these young lives through tithes and financial gifts, helping sponsor missionaries who are called by God to spread the gospel in the Third-World countries.

Especially in a secular world that promotes values contrary to the teachings of Christ Jesus, the local church plays a crucial role.

Becoming spiritual soulmates with your child depends on your commitment to the church as you get involved in worship, study, and service. This involvement and spiritual training early in life will root your child in the Christian faith and give him strength to move into adolescence and adulthood knowing that he is a part of the family of God.

For Christians today, the ultimate worth of all children is in the hands of the local church—Christ's body. Are we giving enough?

SPIRITUAL FOOD FOR THOUGHT

1. Are you a member of a church? How involved are you? Write down specific talents you have. Could any of these be used to the glory of God in your church?

2. Are your children involved in the church's ministry? If not, what would it take for you to make membership a family affair? In what capacities can you volunteer to help your child or teen get involved?

3. Borrow a church hymnal for the week. Go through it with your child and explain denominational traditions, liturgies, and favorite songs.

4. Being part of a spiritual community is vital for faith development. The ritual of worship each week helps children realize they belong to a larger community of Christians. Think of ways to make your family worship experience more meaningful, such as going before the worship service for prayer, explaining the meaning of the stained glass windows, and explaining the different parts of the worship service.

5. Music is an important part of worship. Purchase a tape of favorite hymns and play these for your child. Remind your child of the hymns as they are sung in worship.

Four

Teach Them to Pray

When our children were small, our nightly ritual included praying together before we tucked them in for the night. One night seven-year-old Rob was praying very softly while we sat on the side of his bed with our heads bowed. Bob quietly interrupted the boy's prayer, saying, "Rob, would you speak a bit louder? Mommy and I can't hear you."

Rob opened his wide brown eyes and said matter-of-factly, "But Daddy, I wasn't speaking to you. I was speaking to my other Father."

His relationship had been sealed with his heavenly Father, and we celebrated our son's homecoming!

Prayer can establish your child on the road to a daily, meaningful devotional life. As she takes time from her busy day to be alone with her Father, she will deepen her awareness of God's power in her life. Teaching children to pray begins by *leading the way in our own personal prayer life.* As children see mothers and fathers taking time out of their day to pray, as they hear parents talk about answers to prayer, and as they pray with their parents, they are establishing a "prayer habit" that will continue into Christian adulthood.

LORD, TEACH US TO PRAY

We watched Mother Teresa speak on Robert Schuller's television program several years ago. Dr. Schuller reminded her that the show was being carried all over America and in twenty-two foreign countries, including her native Yugoslavia. He asked her if there was one message she would like to convey to all those viewers. Her response: "Yes, tell them to pray. And tell them to teach their children to pray."

In Mother Teresa's estimation, prayer precedes good works. We must connect with Christ before we can connect with our neighbor.

Jesus' disciples came to Him after He had finished a time apart for prayer, making this request: "Lord, teach us to pray" (Luke 11:1, RSV). Perhaps this is the need of many of us. We could get our lives, our families, and even the world in order . . . if only we knew how to pray.

WHAT IS PRAYER?

Before you can encourage your child to pray regularly with her Father in heaven, you need to understand what prayer is. Fortunately, Jesus has given us a pattern. It begins simply: "Father, hallowed be thy name" (Luke 11:2, RSV).

Prayer is the soul's cry to God for help. Each of us has prayed in moments of distress. Often we haven't recognized this cry as prayer when we said, "Oh God, what am I going to do? How will I make it? Help me, please!" In times of distress, we instinctively reach beyond ourselves for help.

Prayer is the hopes and dreams of all people. Whatever have been your deepest needs have also been your most sincere prayers. What have these been for you? What have the answers been?

Prayer is the peak moments of life. Moments of joy, peace, love, victory . . . those rare moments that come and fill us with wonder, reverence, and humility. These are gifts to be celebrated, and they too are prayers.

Prayer is ongoing communion with God. This is what most of us commonly think of as prayer. This is when we intentionally try to communicate with God.

Prayer is expectancy. One of the great problems of contemporary prayer life is that our prayers lack "expectancy." Do we really believe that God is going to respond? Do we really believe God is going to meet us?

Prayer offers forgiveness. When you pray, God offers forgiveness. Jesus responded to prayer as He said, "Your faith has saved you; go in peace" (Luke 7:50, RSV). Prayer offers us a word of forgiveness from God.

Prayer gives inner strength. When you pray, God stirs you up inside. Look at the Word of God where Isaiah says, "Here am I Lord, send me" (Isa. 6:8, RSV). Prayer offers us new motivation, stirs us up, and gives us inner strength from God.

Prayer gives a sense of purpose. When you pray, God gives direction to life. Jesus said before His crucifixion, burial, and resurrection: "I am the way, the truth, and the life" (John 14:6, RSV). Prayer offers a sense of purpose, a new and authentic clarity about life.

Prayer affirms human existence. Often Jesus withdrew for prayer and meditation. Jesus' concerns covered all of life. Prayer is one of those essential, invisible dimensions of life.

Prayer offers us assurance. When you pray, God speaks a word of ultimate assurance: "Lo, I am with you always" (Matt. 28:20, RSV). One of the things that happened to us in the sixties and seventies was that, in our efforts to change the world, we lost sight of God. While it is important to have deep compassion for our neighbor, we also need to recover the sense of the ultimate Word, that God is in control, and that all is well for those who trust in the Lord. Prayer gives this ultimate hope and assurance from God.

PRAYER REQUIRES COMMITMENT

As you begin to interpret prayer to your child, you must understand that there is a big difference between the tendency to pray and the practice of prayer. We all have the tendency to pray—the crying out in pain, the spontaneous shout of joy. Yet to live a life of prayer is a different story. To pray consistently is *not* easy. It requires commitment and discipline. Don't condemn yourself if you find prayer difficult. Most of us do. Even those we call "saints" told of finding prayer difficult. Read their journals, and you will find them struggling, searching, wrestling, seeking to make the tendency to pray a natural practice in everyday life. Even Jesus' disciples found it difficult to stay awake with Him when He went into the garden to pray.

Prayer is so universal and so natural that its place in our lives needs no defense. We all pray, and we pray because it is a part of our nature. Prayer, however practiced, is related to our search for meaning, our longing for relationship, and our *need* to grow. Prayer is related to our inborn hunger for God. (Prayer is not only for God's benefit, but for ours as well.

The psalmist reminds us of this natural hunger for God: "O God, thou art my God, I seek thee, my soul thirsts for thee; my flesh faints for thee, as in a dry and weary land, where no water is" (Ps. 63:1, RSV). In the Sermon on the Mount, Jesus also recognizes this natural hunger for God: "Blessed are those who hunger and thirst for righteousness, for they shall be satisfied" (Matt. 5:6, RSV).

When we pray, we open our hearts to Jesus. He said, "Apart from me you can do nothing" (John 15:15, RSV). He knew how true these words are, how entirely helpless we are without Him. Yet He also said, "Ask and it will be given you." All you need and more besides. (Matt. 7:7, RSV).

Jesus never grew tired of inviting, prompting, encouraging, admonishing, even commanding us to pray. The many and varied exhortations to pray in the Bible shed remarkable light on prayer.

They show us that prayer is the heartbeat in the life of a saved person.[1]

TEACHING CHILDREN TO PRAY

Prayer is a spiritual discipline in our family. Since our children were infants, we have prayed for them. As they grew into toddlers, we prayed with them and taught them to pray to their heavenly Father. As parents, we model the importance of prayer in our lives. Recently we were looking through some old scrapbooks filled with childhood memorabilia, and we found special prayers that our three children wrote when they were young.

When Rob was age nine, this was his heartfelt prayer:

> "Jesus, please forgive all my sins. I know I've been bad
> and so are my grades. I'd like you to help me pull my
> grades up. Even though I'm a little (or maybe a lot)
> sassy; help me. I love you, me, Mom, Dad, God,
> Brittnye, and Ashley.
> Amen.
> P.S. Do you know where my backpack is?"

A prayer from Ashley, age seven, found scratched on a piece of paper by her bed, simply said:

> "Dear God, please help all the people in our church
> understand what my daddy (Bob) is saying
> from the pulpit.
> Amen."

A most earnest prayer was recorded when Brittnye was just a preschooler:

> "Dear Jesus, I love Mommy, Daddy, Robbie, Ashley, and
> everybody in the whole world! Please help me to beat
> Rob at swimming lessons tomorrow.
> Amen."

When a child prays, he is communicating with God. Like young Rob, Ashley, and Brittnye, most children may not understand this awesome power, but they can experience the comfort and closeness of sharing personal needs with One who cares. They carry with them the hope and faith in a God who loves them and wants to answer their petition. Yet a child cannot experience this relationship with the Father unless someone takes the time to show the way.

Praying with children is a delicate matter. What may seem like a natural form of communication with God must be explained and practiced in a manner children can relate to. Yet many parents don't know where to turn for guidance in teaching their child to pray.

You can begin with the Bible. In this Holy Book, we find Scriptures encouraging us to pray, teaching us how to pray, providing examples of prayer, and giving us answers to our prayers. Mark 2:24 states: "Therefore I tell you, whatever you ask in prayer, believe that you receive it, and it will be yours." John 16:24 (RSV) promises: "Hitherto you have asked nothing in my name; ask, and you will receive, that your joy may be full." Psalm 92:1–2 says: "It is good to give thanks to the Lord . . . to declare thy steadfast love in the morning, and thy faithfulness at night" (RSV).

Prayer played a most important role in the life of Jesus. Wasn't it significant that Jesus prayed at all? Jesus of Nazareth was the Son of God. He had strength of body, strength of mind, strength of purpose and will. He had marvelous strength of affection and strength to move amid the worst conditions. He had strength of patience and was absolutely without fear in the presence of hostility and criticism. He was calm and undaunted when attacked by the official religion of His day. He had every strength we admire in a person, and yet, *Jesus prayed!* He was constantly praying. All of Jesus' life was prayer and love. Christ's life revealed that prayer is not just a pious decoration of life, but the *very breath of human existence.*

Jesus often withdrew for prayer and meditation, prayed all night, and went up on the mountain to pray. He prayed before every important decision in life.

The range of concerns in Jesus' prayers covered all of life—from His changing water into wine at the wedding in Cana at the beginning of His public ministry, to the prayers for His life in Gethsemane at the end. He prayed for the forgiveness of sins for others, prayed over the grave of Lazarus, prayed for the healing of Peter's mother-in-law, and the raising of Jairus' daughter from the dead. The subjects of His prayers included life, health, work, sickness, pain, sin, death, and "all His disciples." No concern of life falls outside the realm of prayer for Jesus—or for us.

When temptation drew near, we find Jesus in prayer. Early in His life, we read that He was tempted to reject the very calling that God had intended. He struggled with Satan over the course His life would take. He knew He could have been powerful, rich, famous. Yet in the wilderness, in prayer, He chose God's way.

YOUR CHILD'S PRAYER LIFE

Using the Bible and the example of Jesus' life of prayer, use the following precepts as you train your children to develop their prayer life with God.

Start Early in Life

Because prayer is a discipline, it is important to start this discipline or training with the youngest children. One of the first words our son learned was at the dinner table when he said "amen" at the end of the family prayer. While many families teach young children prayers such as "God is great. God is good. Let us thank Him for this food," we think children should begin at the youngest age with *prayer as communication.*

Spontaneous prayers that come from the heart can be encouraged, such as "Thank you, God, for this food," or "Thank you,

71

Jesus, for my Mommy and Daddy and new puppy," or, "God, please help my sister to feel better." This early training will enable your child to move into conversational prayer with God in later years. He will view God as a personal Father, someone with whom he can share his most intimate feelings while looking to God for response.

Pray Regularly

In many homes, dinner is the only meal where all the members are present at the table. As our children were growing up, we took advantage of this gathering in our family and encouraged each child to share various joys and concerns with others. When our three teens were at home, each evening a different family member closed this family sharing with a short thank-you prayer to God.

Members bond as they listen to the prayer needs. They experience openness and empathy as real-life struggles. A prayerful environment where God is alive develops as we pause to reflect on the greatness of His bounty.

Teaching children the discipline of prayer each night at the dinner table is not an easy parenting task. Many times in our own home, children have been excused from the table when the words of their prayers have not been appropriate or when holding hands with their siblings turned into an all-out battle. Yet with a *continued loving effort,* family prayer can be taught and have a special meaning to all members.

Once years ago, when the temperatures in our Florida home soared way above the ninety-degree mark, our three children were reacting to the heat and humidity by screaming at each other, name-calling, and an occasional slap or two. As most tired parents do when the summer vacation seems like it will never end, we were continually reprimanding the three for not getting along.

In the midst of the battlefield, the phone rang. *"Take care of Lisa this evening? Of course! Bring her right over."* Mrs. Evans, our neighbor, told of her mother being rushed to the emergency room in a diabetic coma. She needed immediate childcare for her eight-year-old daughter.

After explaining the situation to our three children, we were astonished at the immediate change in dispositions. "Is she going to be OK?" Rob asked tenderly. "Is she going to die?"

"Oh, poor Lisa," Ashley whimpered. "I know she must feel sad."

"I would be so scared if Grandmommy were taken to the hospital. Can't we pray for her?" Brittnye said with empathy in her voice.

Empathy? Tenderness? Prayer? In the midst of uncontrollable fighting, and screaming for their own "space," these children suddenly became sensitive and compassionate young Christians.

Later that evening when we sat down to dinner, the three warriors had changed even more. As we served a large platter of spaghetti, we overheard Brittnye tell Lisa of our family traditions.

"Now, every night at dinner we all join hands and have a family prayer," Brittnye said matter-of-factly as she grabbed the hand of the younger child, then took the hand of her brother. "And then we go around the table and pray for someone who needs help."

"Yeah. You can pray for your grandmommy," Ashley chimed in.

"We *all* will pray for her grandmother," my oldest son added wisely.

Were these the same three children who had grumbled and groaned when their father reminded them of our family prayer the night before? Were they actually joining hands in love instead of refusing to touch each other during the prayer?

Yes, the discipline of family prayer can work! Yet loving Christian parents must make the time to instill this ritual into the family's regular routine.

Join Your Children When They Pray

Bedtime prayer is another ritual in our home. At this time, conversation with God is shared between parent and each child. An aura of peaceful solitude descends as a child kneels beside his bed and talks to his heavenly Father.

Instead of merely reminding your children to pray, be there with them as they converse with God and establish the habit of communication with God. As our children grew older, a devotional book and Bible by their bed enabled them to continue this discipline of bedtime prayer.

Speak in a Child's Language

A missionary from overseas stayed in our home several years ago. During his visit we asked him to pray before our meal. His words were beautifully spoken as he added Scripture and meaningful prayer language. One could tell the young man experienced a true personal relationship with God. Yet some of his terms, such as "thee" and "magnify" or references to Jesus as "the light," went completely over the head of our youngest child. The missionary in our home used prayer words that were too abstract for young children. Prayers for children must be simple.

Let your child know that talking to God is like talking to a dear friend. God is strong like a father, gentle like a mother. He is all-caring and wants to know our innermost thoughts, fears, and dreams. Yet your child doesn't have to use impressive words to get God's attention; honesty and oneness are much more important. Abstract terms add only to the confusion and unnecessary mystery to our faith.

Don't Use Prayer as a Form of Reprimand

Sometimes, after an especially trying day, we have been tempted to say, "Please, Lord, help my sweet daughter to be more obedient," or "God, you know how much our son needs to watch his language," while praying with the children. Yet, prayer is between a person and God, and not to be used as a gimmick for disciplining others.

Some parents use prayer as a form of punishment. At a Bible study several years ago, a young woman shared that her mother would make the most disobedient child in the family pray at dinner each evening. The result? "We grew up hating to pray," she said. "To this day, I still fear closing my eyes and being alone with God."

Thank God for Your Child

Thanking God openly for your child helps to affirm his importance as a member of the family and a child of God. At dinnertime, we lift up each family member to God, thanking God for his or her uniqueness. The simple but profound phrase, "Thank You, God, for [person's name]," gives each person a feeling of worth and spiritual wholeness.

Practice Spontaneous Prayers

Spontaneous prayers throughout the day can help a child recognize the love of God in his life. Verbally acknowledging the beauty of a sunrise, the opening bud on the rosebush, or the first raindrop on a cloudy day can enhance your child's relationship with God. While we need to remember the sick, the sorrowing, the hungry, and troubled, we also need to pray when times are good. Words of thankfulness and gratitude add a bright dimension to one's prayer life.[2]

Explain Prayer Formulas

You also can explain different prayer "formulas" that can help your child get focused as he prays. One formula, A.C.T.S., speaks of the different components of prayer, such as Adoration or praise, Confession and asking for forgiveness, Thanksgiving, and Supplication or petitions for self and others. Ask your child to think of specific prayers in each category:

A doration (praising God) _____

C onfession (of wrong behavior and sins): _____

T hanksgiving _____

S upplication (requests for self and others): _____

Some people like to use another formula called "J.O.Y." This acronym breaks prayer down into three categories: praying to Jesus, praying for Others, then praying for Yourself. Talk with your child about both methods of praying and see if these may help him get started.

J oy (praying to Jesus): _____

O thers (supplication): _____

Y ourself (petitions): _____

Be Creative When You Pray

A simple song can be a powerful prayer, if the attitude is right. Singing songs such as "Jesus Loves Me," "God Cares about You," "God Is So Good," or "Pass It On" with your children can be a meaningful prayertime. A litany describing feelings on a specific topic can be read by all family members, or a Scripture that pertains to a family situation can be read as a prayer. By not limiting the types of prayer, we can expand the ways we teach our children to talk with God.

Listen to God

Teach your child to listen to God during prayertime. How can we hear God's voice? Let your child know that we have intuitions that are from God, such as when we think, "That is a good way to act" or "That will get me in trouble." Through intuitions, Scriptures, and our conscience, God speaks to us.

Older children can become aware of God's voice speaking through personal quiet time, worship services, prayer and meditation, Bible reading; and other Christians, such as pastors, parents, older siblings, or grandparents. Give your child a notebook to write down any thoughts she feels are from God.

HOW DOES GOD ANSWER PRAYER?

"But why did she die?" our daughter asked. "I prayed for Ginger to get well. Why did she have to die?" One of your most difficult tasks as a parent is helping your child cope with situations that don't seem fair. From praying for health and not getting well, to praying for a kitten and not receiving one, children can feel the disappointment of what they believe is unanswered prayer.

God has many ways to answer prayers. He promises to hear every word you and I utter to Him. If we are obedient children, He responds in a way that is best *over the long haul* for us and for His glory. We must trust Him.

We have a right to come into the presence of God, expecting that He will hear and expecting that He will answer in a way that will reflect His glory and fulfill His will and help us grow in Him. God has told us to expect spiritual joy and liberation when we enter His presence. If we come into His presence expecting "showers of blessing," we will walk away drenched with what God wants to give us. It's been said that if you come into the presence of God with only a tin cup, you'll only receive enough to fill it. Yet if you come expectantly with a bucket, then *God has placed Himself under divine obligation to give you what you came to get.*

TOUCH COMMUNICATES CARING

Touch communicates caring to your child during prayer. At the dinner table, we join hands symbolizing the unbroken circle of God's love in our family. At other times, a hand on the shoulder relates the same love and concern.

A study was performed at the library of a large northeastern university. As students checked out books, library workers were asked to touch half of the students in some way—shaking their hand or patting their arm or back. The other students weren't touched at all. As the students left the library, a survey was taken with the question, "What do you think of the university's library?" The students who had been touched in some way all spoke highly of the library services, while the students who were not touched told of its inadequacies or were apathetic. The point is that touch brings positive feelings.

Jesus used touch during His ministry to bless and heal those around Him. We can follow Christ's example by a simple hug or pat on the back after a bedtime prayer. A bond forms between parent, child, and God as physical affection is expressed.

Prayer Lists, Prayer Partners, Prayer Time

Encourage your child to write down his petitions for prayer, then to check them off as answers are given—even if the answer is "no." You may keep an ongoing prayer list taped to your refrigerator door for family members to add to and check off as needed.

Establish prayer partners in your household. You might choose names out of a box each week so each member prays for a different family member that week. Talk about the feelings we have when someone prays for us and with us. Are our lives changed when people pray for us consistently?

Set a certain prayer time within your day to pray with your child. Whether this is at dinner time, bed time or before school, let this become a ritual your child can count on and grow from.

Establish a Prayer Box

Put a small box on the kitchen table with blank pieces of paper and a pen nearby. Ask family members to write down specific prayer requests and put them in the prayer box. Each evening, use these requests as the basis for your family prayer.

Use Sentence Prayers throughout the Day

Teach your child that his life can be a prayer as he prays throughout the day. When he feels grateful, teach him to tell God with a brief sentence such as, "Thank You, God." When he is nervous before a soccer game or a test, a quick "God be with me" or "God give me strength" can offer peace of mind.

Expect Miracles

Prayer is communication with a loving God. Answers to prayer should always be expected. Bring an atmosphere of anticipation to your family as you pray together. Share answers to prayer you have experienced and encourage your children to do the same. A prayer list on a sheet of paper will help members see how God meets requests. Check the names and concerns from time to time, and discuss the miracle of prayer.

Does God Say No?

The essence of prayer is to put ourselves on God's side—not try to put God on our side. This means we must try to get in tune with God's will for our lives instead of trying to talk God into succumbing to our will. While we pray for our needs and desires, we have to remember that God has a plan for our lives and doesn't always answer our way. Remember, teach your child, "Thy will be done," not "my will be done." That's not an easy concept for most children, who view God as a type of "Santa Claus."

TEACHING TEENS TO PRAY

"Sometimes I don't know what to say when I talk with God. What do you say?"

Our teenage daughter popped this question while we were sitting in the yard watching a brilliant Florida sunset last summer. Her query reminded us of the disciples as they asked Jesus for guidance in praying to their heavenly Father. Most parents want their teens to have a personal relationship with God. This awareness that God knows them, cares about them, and has a plan for their lives can be a reality as you take time to teach your teen how to pray.

Make Plans to Be Together

A warm afternoon spent out-of-doors with your teen is a perfect time to begin this teaching. You can both sit on a blanket under a shade tree, take a picnic supper to a nearby park, or go anywhere that's conducive to being at one with God. You can prepare by reading this chapter and then doing the suggested *family time* activities with your teen.

Set the Mood

If your teens are like ours, they aren't always going to be in a frame of mind to talk about something as personal as their prayer life. Teens often don't feel like praying or don't think they need to pray. To some, praying aloud or even admitting to Mom or Dad that they pray is embarrassing. You may have to wait for "signals" from them, such as:

- questions they have regarding God and prayer

- disappointments or sadness they faced

- unanswered prayers or answers they didn't ask for

Choose a time when your teen is in a congenial mood, then suggest that he spend some quiet time with you.

Begin with the Bible

As you give your teen suggestions for praying, begin with the Bible. In this Holy Book, we find verses encouraging us to pray, teaching us how to pray, providing examples of prayer, and giving us answers to our prayers. Remember Mark 11:24: "Therefore I tell you, whatever you ask in prayer, believe that you have received it, and it will be yours" (RSV).

Encourage Personal Sharing

Tell your teen that God wants to know all about the concerns, needs, and problems he may have. Personal joys can include answers to prayers, goals met, or relationships that have been enhanced. Concerns include praying for those who are ill, personal stumbling blocks, or unresolved conflicts with friends.

Ask your teen: "If you could pray for two things, what would you say?" Help him express himself in a manner that is comfortable, genuine, and appropriate. Talk with him about his prayer as conversation with God until he feels comfortable in saying the words aloud.

Often teens have a difficult time expressing their feelings openly with God. You can help your teen (or older child) learn to do this by giving him some open-ended sentences and asking him to fill in the blanks silently. For example:

- I am happy about _____.

- I am thankful for _____.

- I am sad about _____.

- I worry about _____.

- I want to pray for _____.

Talk about Answers

As you talk with your teen about prayer, emphasize that God loves us, and He understands when we are sad or frustrated by something that seems unfair. Acknowledge that you don't have all the answers, saying, "I don't know why, but I do know God loves us." Let your teen know that God answers prayers in many ways. He may say, *Yes, No, Maybe, Wait,* or *I'm going to surprise you.*

Yes is the obvious answer we want to hear when we pray. Yet you can talk with your teen about other answers God gives. While we should pray for what we want, we must realize that God knows us better than we know ourselves, and He knows what is best for our life.

How does your teen view prayer? Ask: Which of these statements do you believe to be true about your prayers?

_____ God hears my prayers and answers them.

_____ I only pray when I am sad or frightened.

_____ Some things are too unimportant to bother God with.

_____ God doesn't always answer my prayers.

_____ God doesn't always hear what I am saying.

_____ I shouldn't have to pray if God knows all.

Let your teen know that everything—the good and the bad—is important to God, and He hears and answers all prayers.

God wants us to pray because it establishes a relationship with Him, just as our friends need us to talk to them. Even though God's answers to our prayers may differ from our expectations, we need to bring *everything in prayer* to Him.

With your teen, compile a family prayer list of specific needs or requests, and family members can lift these up in personal devotion time. Hang the prayer list up in the kitchen so all can see it, and cross off answers to prayer as they occur.

HOW THEN SHALL WE PRAY?

Encourage your children or teens to pray spontaneously throughout the day as they recognize the love of God in their lives. Encourage them to see prayer not as a series of requests but as a way of life, a oneness with God. Model prayer as ongoing communication as you talk of God's love. Your child will learn that prayer is not just a two-minute activity, but a day-in, day-out relationship with a loving Father.

SPIRITUAL FOOD FOR THOUGHT

1. How would you describe God? Some terms that come to mind are a loving parent, hallowed, holy, revered, awe-inspiring, the source of our life, the everlasting Hope. Without God, we would not exist. Acknowledge God's presence in your life with a prayer each day this week.

2. Use the prayer formulas given on page 76 to pray with your child this week. Write these on a sheet of paper and let your child fill in the blanks.

3. Talk about forgiveness with your child. Isn't it easy to show anger but difficult to show forgiveness? Forgiveness requires the grace of God. We are able to forgive because we have experienced forgiveness ourselves. Include prayers for forgiveness in your prayer time this week.

4. Through prayer, God reveals His will for our lives and places His thoughts into our minds. Write down thoughts that you feel are of God and share these with someone this week.

5. Keep a prayer list where family members can see it. Ask each member to write down names or situations in need of prayer. Check off those answers to prayer. Talk about how God chose to answer these, using the information on page 77.

Five

Develop Spiritual Discipline

A young friend came over to our home last summer and told us he had accepted Christ into his life. We rejoiced with this teen and were genuinely excited because we had been praying for him for several years. After he told us about his new life with Christ, he seemed confused, saying, "I know that I'm a Christian, but how am I supposed to live? Does this change me in any way?"

To begin with, becoming a Christian and learning to live like Christ are two different matters. When we become Christians, we acknowledge our innermost desire to ask Jesus Christ to live within us and be the Lord of our lives. Yet to learn about God through Jesus Christ and to grow spiritually, we must make time every day for Bible study, prayer, meditation, and personal reflection. Our children can only do this if we make spiritual discipline a priority in the home.

Discipline comes from a word that has the same Latin root as disciple, which means to "teach and guide." Most of us understand the biblical mandate to take control in the home by "disciplining" our children. Yet did you know that we also must discipline our children in their spiritual development? When a daily quiet time with God becomes a discipline in the early years, a child will carry this with him into teenage years and adulthood. As our children started a devotional habit of Bible reading, memorization of key verses, understanding the Scriptures, and developing a prayer relationship with God, they strengthened their internal life.

Discipline is variously defined as training intended to produce a pattern of behavior or the behavior resulting from such training. From another perspective, discipline can be seen as punishment intended to correct or train, or a set of rules or methods. In the context of the Christian faith, however, a disciple is not just one who subscribes to the teachings of Jesus and seeks to spread them, but one who seeks to "relive" Jesus' life in the world. Discipline for the Christian is the way we train ourselves, or allow the Spirit to train us, to be "like Jesus," to appropriate His Spirit, and to cultivate His power to live His life in the world.[1]

How to Develop the Devotional Habit

Remember that the more disciplined you are in helping your child develop a devotional habit—spending time regularly with God—the more certain you can be that your child will incorporate this training into his daily routine. Yet it's not easy to establish spiritual disciplines today. It often seems that just when we have our child's attention for family devotionals, Bible stories, or praying together, the phone rings loudly, someone knocks at the door, or an enticing commercial blasts on the television.

Parents can encourage their children in several ways to pause from the busy world we live in as they set aside daily time alone and develop a devotional habit.

Make Time to Be Alone

The Gospels have given us a wealth of insight into the beauty of solitude. Being alone, as indicated by the life of Jesus, need not be a time for feeling sorry for oneself. It can be a time for finding meaning in one's life. In solitude, Jesus found His source of power. After spending the day preaching to and teaching the crowds, He "went up into a mountain apart to pray" (Matt. 14:23, KJV). Luke told of Jesus spending time teaching and nurturing the people, then He "withdrew himself into the wilderness, and prayed" (Luke 5:16, KJV).

Our children can find this unending source of strength, renewal, and encouragement as they follow the example of our Lord and retreat to solitude—their bedroom, a quiet place in the living room or den, or outside. As they learn to listen to God through prayer, study, and thought, they will discover their own inner resources and use them to witness of God's grace to those around them.

It was in 1882 on the campus of Cambridge University in England that the world was first given the slogan: "Remember the morning watch." Christian students found their days loaded with studies, lectures, games, and bull sessions. Enthusiasm and activity were the order of the day. These dedicated men soon discovered a flaw in their spiritual armor—a small crack that if not soon closed would bring disaster. They sought an answer and came up with a scheme they called the "morning watch"—a plan to spend the first minutes of each new day alone with God, praying and reading the Bible.

The "morning watch" scaled the crack. It enshrined a truth so often obscured by the pressure of ceaseless activity that it needs daily rediscovery: To know God, it is necessary to spend consistent time with Him.[2]

In Romans, Paul affirms taking "time out" to be alone and teaches us to ignore the cries of the world as we focus on a daily devotional habit with our children.

Time spent with God in devotion needs to become a daily habit. Encourage your child to choose a time, perhaps before school or before bedtime, to spend at least five minutes alone with God.

Purchase a Children's Bible

Make sure your child has an age-appropriate Bible, and encourage her to read Scriptures during devotion time. The Gospel of John is an excellent book to start with; it's easy to understand and focuses on Jesus' unity with God. Urge your child to circle or underline favorite verses. The Bible is the one Book that must be "worn" to be effective in the life of the reader. Georgianna Summers, in *Teaching as Jesus Taught*, suggests that children place an exclamation point (!) on ideas that they find exciting, a question mark (?) on ideas that need clarification, an upward arrow (↟) on anything that seems to tell them "Do this," and a downward arrow (↡) for the message, "Stop doing this."[3]

Choose a children's Bible or devotional book that appeals to you and your child. Here are some suggestions:

- *The Beginner's Bible,* a picture Bible storybook by Karyn Henley (Questar, 1989)

- *Leading Little Ones to God,* by Marian Schoolland (Eerdman's, 1981)

- *Big Thoughts for Little People,* based on concepts from the Book of Proverbs, by Kenneth Taylor (Tyndale, 1983)

- *Giant Steps for Little People,* from the Sermon on the Mount, by Kenneth Taylor (Tyndale, 1985).

- *Adventures in the Big Thicket,* by Ken Gire (Focus on the Family, 1990)

- *Growing Up Together, Devotions for Mom and Me,* an activity-oriented, topical study, including a calendar and activity book with a spiritual concept to digest each month, by Jan Kempe (Discovery House, 1989)[4]

- *Jesus for Little Ones,* by Charles Foster (Broadman & Holman, 1994).

Encourage Ongoing Prayer

Explain different prayer "formulas" (as explained in Chapter 4) that can help your child get focused as he prays, such as "J.O.Y" *(praying to Jesus, praying for Others, then praying for Yourself)* and "A.C.T.S." *(Affirmation, Confession, Thanksgiving, Supplication)*.

Keep a Spiritual Journal

Give your child a colorful notebook and bright markers to keep a list of prayer requests, and teach her how to write down notes as God answers these prayers. Encourage her to keep this notebook with her Bible and to use it as a daily journal of spiritual thoughts. If the child is unable to write, let her talk to you and share her feelings and thoughts. Keep these in her daily journal and share them with her in later years.

Suggest Seeking God's Guidance

As your child tells of worries and fears, encourage him to turn them over to God during his prayer time. You might suggest, "Why don't you pray to God and ask for help?" or, "Perhaps God will give you the answer. Let's pray about this." Help him develop a habit of turning to the Lord during times of trial and adversity as he matures.

Lead the Way

Again, parents should lead the way as they spend time daily with God through personal devotions. This time out for renewal can give inspiration, strength, knowledge, and insight into Christian living as parents and children strive for a deeper faith. Let your child see you having quiet time, and let her know that reading the Bible and praying to God each day are very important to you.

TEENS AND DEVOTIONS

Many parents tell of having no problem getting preschoolers and elementary-school-age children to focus on daily devotional time. Yet what about the teenage years? We speak from the experience of having reared three very active teens. We have done our best to encourage their daily quiet time so they can pray, study the Bible, and be at one with God. But let's face it; it's not always easy to stay on top of a busy teen's spiritual development—especially when her calendar is filled with school activities, friends, and part-time jobs. What's the solution? You can help continue her spiritual and faith development with some meaningful ways to "let the Son shine in."

Keep a Personal Diary

A personal diary can help your teen plot her spiritual journey and discover her inner self. Each day she can assess her spiritual attitude, learn how the highs and lows of contemporary life affect her emotionally, and witness how God is moving in her life. This writing will capture her deepest feelings—thoughts she might not even share with a best friend or parent.

A personal diary can help a busy teen get organized for spiritual growth as she documents feelings and thoughts each day. She can look back over the journal weeks later and see her faith at its highs and lows, peaks and valleys. The journal also can become an intimate place where she can ventilate, meditate, solve problems, and dream—without feeling threatened or intimidated.

Suggest that your teen write down thoughts during a quiet time each day of what she feels God is saying to her. Let her know that we hear God through Bible study, other Christians, and during time alone as we pray and listen to His "still small voice." In the journal your teen can keep prayer lists, write down answers to prayers, and set spiritual study goals. Encourage your teen to open up her imagination, to reflect deeply about her spiritual life as she keeps this journal. She can get in touch with her inner spirit as she becomes more aware of God working through and around her.

Encourage Time for Prayer and Meditation

Too many of us try to intellectualize our lives, but the soul is not an intellectual structure. We participate in spirituality; it involves living fully. Encourage your teen to become intimate with his soul as he observes the world around him and begins to see it from a spiritual realm.

The Roman Emperor and philosopher Marcus Aurelius said, "A man's life is what his thoughts make it." Prayer and meditation will help your teen's mind take a break from daily school work and other routines while giving support to the spiritual dimension of life. Prayer nurtures the ongoing personal relationship between your teen and God; times of meditation and aloneness allow him to learn "who he is and whose he is." Through prayer and meditation, your teen can excuse himself from daily problems and focus on his inner will and creative spirit. This time away from the mundane will allow your teen's body, mind, and spirit to experience healing.

With prayer or meditation, he can get in touch with his inner needs and learn to hear God speaking in his life. This knowledge of "self" will be most important as he gets in touch with his spiritual nature and with God. When he feels as if his world is caving in around him and he longs for a fortress to give him refuge, prayer and mediation will enable him to find an unshakable source of strength.

Name Spiritual Experiences

Teach your teen to get into the habit of naming her daily spiritual experiences by reflecting on these questions:

What did I do today that was of God?

- helped a friend
- volunteered at school

- comforted a sibling
- listened to a parent

What did I see today that was of God?

- the flower blooming
- the smiles of friends
- the cloudless sky
- the bright summer sun

What did I think today that was of God?

- loving thoughts
- empathetic thoughts
- thoughts of concern
- benevolent thoughts

You might involve the entire family in this spiritual reflection and ask the questions listed above at dinner time. Encourage all members to stay in tune with their spiritual nature as they look for God in all of life.

Set Spiritual Goals

Purchase a calendar for your teen to write down these spiritual study goals. Most teens are busy writing dates and school activities on their calendar, but keeping track of spiritual growth is more important. On the calendar, your teen can write down the specific Scriptures he wants to study during the upcoming month, then check off each day as he follows through. If he memorizes a verse, suggest that he write this on the calendar in colored ink so he can refer to it later.

Purchase a Youth Bible

Make sure your teen has an easy-to-understand youth Bible, and encourage her to circle or underline favorite verses each day with colored markers.

Some excellent Bibles for teens include:

- *The Youth Bible*, New Century Version (Word Publishing, 1991).

The Youth Bible has easy-to-read Bible text translated into modern English, topical devotions that relate the Bible to the everyday life of a teenager, and sidelight boxes that provide insight and fun facts about life in biblical times.

- *Life Application Bible for Students*, The Living Bible (Tyndale House Publishers, Inc., 1992). The *Life Application Bible for Students* has profiles of biblical personalities that highlight how they were human, with strengths and weaknesses, and life application notes on almost every page that tell teens how to put biblical passages into practice.

- *The Student Bible*, New International Version (Zondervan Publishing House, 1986). *The Student Bible* includes special life questions, helping to relate passages to real-life situations for teens, and helpful notes, called "Highlights," that explain confusing verses.

Provide Devotional Books

Provide your teen with a new youth devotional book that speaks to him about a living faith in God. Some suggested books for preteens and teens include:

- *Falling Off Cloud Nine and Other High Places*, Lorraine Peterson, Bethany House.

- *Anybody Can Be Cool But Awesome Takes Practice*, Lorraine Peterson, Bethany House.

- *How to Stay Way Cool When Things Are Tough*, Susan Nally, Broadman & Holman.

- *How to Say Yes! to all the Right Choices (and Really Mean It)*, Susan Nally, Broadman & Holman Publishers.

- *How to Feel Most Excellent About Who You Are (and Really Enjoy It)*, Susan Nally and Liz Lee, Broadman & Holman Publishers.

- *How to Have a Radical Attitude Toward God (and Really Believe It)*, Liz Lee, Broadman & Holman Publishers.

All resources are available at most Christian bookstores or can be ordered.

Let the Son Shine In

Suggest to your teen that she have her daily quiet time out-of-doors, if the weather permits, during her favorite time of day. Plan a family time each weekend where personal faith and feelings are shared between parents and teens. This relaxed quiet time can also be held out-of-doors in your back yard or a local lake or park. In the winter months, celebrate family time indoors. Tell your teen how God has blessed you that week, and share personal stories about faith struggles and the peace you have received through Jesus Christ.

Setting aside time each day to be alone with God in prayer, meditation, Bible study, and journaling allows us to be in communion with God, to feel His presence, and to seek His guidance in our daily lives. If you have a strong devotional life, you know the strength and power it adds to your daily routine—especially when trials and troubles hit.

Not only does our devotional habit mean bringing our personal problems and fears to God, it means learning to trust God to take these fears away and replace them with faith. We must teach our children that personal devotional time is not only for daily renewal but also for strength in coping with the demands of a secular society. This time will help them cope with the adversities of childhood and the loneliness of adolescence as they place their confidence in the Lord.

HAVING FAMILY DEVOTIONALS

An important spiritual ritual in our home is a regular family devotional. This time is specifically set aside to allow members to slow down and come together as a family. The devotions include reading Scriptures, discussing their meaning, sharing personal concerns, singing, and talking about God. It is a time when your family can establish firmer roots in Christ.

A meaningful devotional in the home depends on your enthusiasm. You can open the door to inspiration if you are excited about your faith and radiate this to your children.

Spend Time with Your Child

Before you begin with the ritual of daily family devotionals, spend time each day alone with your children. Talk about their perception of faith—their struggles, dreams, and goals. Ask questions about their personal likes and dislikes, and listen! Leading a devotional with your family is not difficult. See the possibilities of sharing a living Lord, building deeper relationships, affirming your children, and lovingly involving them in a spiritual learning experience.

Read the Scriptures Ahead of Time

Preparation before having a family devotional involves knowing your subject. Search in prayer and Bible study for answers to problems your children may be having. Read verses that apply to these concerns ahead of time. Think of discussion questions that relate to the verses presented and also to your children. How does the Scripture relate to problems they may be having with peers, at school, or at home?

Prepare open-ended questions for your family devotional that call for expressing feelings, ideas, and creative thoughts. Try to avoid using questions that require only a yes or no answer. One way you can do this is to ask, "How would you feel if this happened to you?"

or "Why do you feel he did that?" Allow for a flow of personal opinions and ideas—answers that are neither right nor wrong.

An excellent Bible from Broadman & Holman Publishers is the *Family Worship Bible* for family devotions. It offers page after page of helps designed to deepen your family's relationship not only with God but also with each other.

Have Fair Rules for Discussion

In a family devotional, have the rule that "all is OK" as you encourage all members to speak their opinion. Comments made as the different members speak, such as "very interesting" or "I like that idea," will stimulate discussion. This builds up a child and encourages more participation.

Refrain from being critical in your family devotion, even if the idea your child shares is totally irrelevant. Rather, use each statement and build on it. Comments such as "That may be true; can anyone else add another thought?" or "That may be one way of looking at it, but how does it apply to the Scripture we are studying?" help rescue the discussion from bogging down. This also saves the child from unnecessary embarrassment.

Look beyond the Words

Observe your child during the family devotional. Watch for body language that may be telling the opposite of what the child is saying. If she is relating feelings of peacefulness and security, yet is nervously sitting on the chair, twitching and shaking, she might be crying out for caring. Again, you have the responsibility to affirm, to build up, and to encourage the child as you nurture spiritual development.

Emphasize the Gospel Message

Is there a lull in the conversation? Has your family devotional reached a peak but not a conclusion? Now is the time to bring the message of the Gospels. Have Scripture ready to share with your children relating to the discussion topic. Tell of your own encounters with God through Jesus Christ. Relate these discussion topics to your personal faith story. By sharing your own ups and downs, your struggles and victories, you can help children learn what it means to follow Christ and grow as Christians.

Be Creative

Is your child musical? artistic? dramatic? Some children may respond to lyrics in contemporary Christian songs during family worship, while others may enjoy acting out a Bible story. By knowing your child's talents and interests, you can gear the family devotional in a creative manner that meets his needs and attracts his attention.

Consider the uniqueness of your child, his level of maturity, and his personal knowledge about the devotional topic. A preschooler reacts differently to a story about salvation than would an early teen. A verse about *agape* love has different meanings for an immature six-year-old and a mature sixteen-year-old.

Clay modeling, wire sculpting, and painting are excellent ways to involve the entire family during devotionals. Still they don't lend themselves to every subject discussed. These props are best used when feelings need to be expressed.

Often, if a devotional is about a new land in the Bible or a new group of people, pictures of these places and people make appropriate props. Illustrations of biblical geography and culture can be found in picture book versions of the Bible story, in Sunday school curriculum materials, or in Bible atlases and handbooks. As your child sees what you are talking about, he is more likely to learn it.

Use Creative Worship Supplies

Keep the following on hand to use during family worship to help your child express his thoughts and feelings creatively.

- modeling clay   chalk
- wire for sculpting   glue
- tape recorder and blank tapes   scissors
- video camera and blank tapes   maps
- scraps of fabric   markers
- burlap for making banners   paper
- old magazines   tape
- biblical pictures or photographs

TAKE ONE DAY AT A TIME

While establishing the spiritual discipline of daily quiet time and family devotionals isn't always easy, the rewards are great. Instead of incorporating every suggestion in this chapter in one day, start with one daily action. Once your child enjoys her new Bible or finds it enlightening to keep a daily journal, then tackle another suggestion or action. What we are challenging you to do is to substitute new "spiritual" behaviors for old habits, such as watching television or playing video games. As your child learns these new habits, challenge her to practice them daily, and watch her spiritual growth blossom.

SPIRITUAL FOOD FOR THOUGHT

1. Do you find it hard to hold family devotionals with your children? What obstacles do you face? How do your children respond to prayer and Bible reading as a family? What about teens?

2. Try having a family devotional each night this week. Follow the suggestions in this chapter, and write down in your journal your children's responses.

3. Teach your child that everything we need comes from God. Write down five of your child's daily needs or ask her to do this.

4. Emphasize to your child that God will take care of his needs, and that he must be sensitive to this. God may also use him to meet the needs of someone else. For example, a friend at school may be feeling lonely, and God may want him to befriend this person. Or, his sister may need help with her homework, and God wants him to use his talents to help her. We need to stay aware of the needs of others and think about how God may use us to fulfill them.

5. What needs do your friends have this week? Family members? Try to be sensitive to the intimate needs of those around you and let God love them through you.

Six

See God Every Day

We'll never forget when Ashley was four years old. She was always quite analytical in thinking about life and faith, always wanting to know who God was and how we knew God was there. One rainy evening at dusk, we walked by Ashley's room and noticed her sitting on the bed, daydreaming out the window while "talking" to God. In her tiniest preschooler voice, Ashley whispered, "God is very big, God is very small. God is high, God is low. God is very happy, and God is very sad."

Then she paused for a minute, without noticing that we were listening, and added with great soul-searching: "I love God . . . but God scares me."

"God is mysterious," Brittnye commented after we shared Ashley's interesting insights later that evening with our older children. "How do we really know that God is present in our lives?" In his book, *Talking to Your Child about God*, David Heller writes that looking for God is like searching for a white pearl in the snow. You know it's there somewhere, but it blends in so perfectly with the scenery that it's difficult to grasp. The mystery and intangibility of God has puzzled man since the beginning of time, but it is a mystery that can be solved . . . if you look for "signs" of God's love in your daily actions.

Finding a sense of the sacred is difficult when we live in such a "techno-society." The noise and activity of this world relentlessly presses in on us. For many of us, any "down time" is spent doing just that—sleeping, dozing, or sitting and watching TV. *Yet spirituality must involve our entire being!* For our children to grow up knowing the ever-present reality of a God who cares for all humankind, we must lead the way daily to see God as He intimately touches our lives.

How do you explain love to your child? This is an invisible and mysterious thing, yet you know it exists! You describe love through the "eyes of your soul," relating personal experiences, intimate feelings, and changed lives from being loved and sharing love.

How do we explain God in our everyday lives? The answer is the same. You tell your children what you have seen through the "eyes of your soul." We must teach our children to see the world around us from a spiritual perspective. Spiritual experiences emerge from the most unexpected places. They surprise us, and we often recognize them only in retrospect. Spiritual lessons can take place while gardening, sitting at the beach, and playing with children, as well as attending worship.[1]

As you see God in life's experiences and share these moments with your child, you will help to awaken her spirituality. Taking time to watch the delicate hummingbird feed on the honeysuckle's sweet nectar, observing the ominous clouds before a thunderstorm, or standing in awe at the birth of a kitten, you can share messages about God and His plan for all creation.

GOD'S CREATION IS OUR SOURCE OF JOY

Throughout this chapter we will suggest ideas and activities for you to try with your child as you guide him to a greater awareness of God's creation. Incorporate these ideas into your daily life instead of forcing them upon your child. You are not trying to teach or lecture your child about the reality of God. Rather, your ultimate goal is for your child to become acutely aware of the presence and wonder of God in everyday life—in His world. With that in mind, you can celebrate the divine, the whimsical, the momentary, the daily—*with your child*—so that God becomes more than a word spoken on Sunday morning. He becomes present in your child's every breath.

Telling your younger child that God is love can be very confusing. But when you spend family time together on a regular basis, the message of a loving God will become real as you make statements such as, "God gave us a beautiful sunny day so we can go outside and ride bikes," or "Aunt Lori's new baby is a precious gift from God," or "I thank God for you every day!" or "God has blessed you with the most wonderful friends!" Such statements help to establish a connection between God and nature, God and love, and God and the child.

Celebrate God's World

The Christian faith is one to be celebrated, and nature is full of this energy, wonder, and joy. Through endless oceans, towering trees, majestic mountains, and calming sunsets, we can see examples of God's creation and His power. When we share these marvels with our children, we affirm that all things are created by God for His world.

Throughout the Bible are Scriptures telling of the majesty and wonder of God's creation. As you embark on a spiritual journey with your child, you can capture this *spirit of celebration* and live it daily. When you go on a walk with your child, do so with anticipation of seeing the wonders of God's kingdom on earth. When it begins to rain, go outside, lift your hands to the heavens, and show your child how to taste the warm raindrops as you celebrate this nourishment for God's beautiful earth. At the beach or lake, splash in the water joyfully with your child as you enjoy the gift of water to sustain life.

Sense God's World

As parents, we can help reveal God's love to our children as they open their senses to nature. Teach your children to be grateful for healthy air, fresh water, green forests, and healthful foods. The senses unlock the door to a great learning experience for kids. Children seem to have a built-in drive to taste, to see, to hear, to smell and feel, to totally absorb what they are investigating.[2] When learners of all ages get involved in learning God's Word as well as application of the Bible in daily living, they need to use as many of the senses as possible.[3]

Consider the excitement of learning your child will have as he opens his senses to enhance and add variety to seeing God in everyday life!

How can you help your child awaken his senses?

See God's Wonder

Take your child outside and show him

- sunsets and sunrises

- birds in the air and blue skies

- green grass

- babies with loving parents

- a colorful rainbow

- the bright summer sun

- waves crashing on the beach

- friends at play

- a new puppy

- trees bending during a storm

Hear God's Wonder

Teach her to be aware of

- lyrical music
- rain on the roof
- birds singing
- leaves rustling in the wind
- the wind whistling on a stormy night
- thunder clapping in the night's sky
- crickets chirping at dark
- frogs singing
- babies crying
- children laughing
- the pastor preaching
- the organ playing
- the choir singing
- bells ringing

Touch God's Wonder

Let him touch

- wind blowing
- icy snow
- rough bark on a tree
- cool water in a stream
- wet grass
- thick, muddy soil

- a fluffy kitten
- a baby's velvety skin
- leaves on a tree
- ripples in a seashell
- warm rain

Smell God's Wonder

Show her God's wonder as she smells

- sea air
- a lawn freshly cut
- sweet scents of spring
- freshly cut fruit
- a pine cone
- spices, such as cinnamon or cloves
- the air after a rainstorm
- freshly cut roses
- mint leaves

Taste God's Wonder

Awaken his taste to God's creation with

- the crispness of an apple
- a juicy orange
- the softness of a banana
- creamy milk
- a sour lemon
- salty ocean water.

EACH DAY IS A GIFT FROM GOD

To nurture your child's spiritual development, help her to understand that each day is a gift from God—from waking up in the morning to the sounds of birds greeting the new dawn, to the smells of a hot breakfast, to feeling the love of a parent's good-morning hug, to tasting the icy glass of juice, to seeing the vivid blue sky . . . your child can learn to sense God's presence and heighten her awareness of a greater power in her life. As you make time to awaken your child's senses through learning and praise experiences, she will begin to understand that all of the earthly treasures are gifts from her heavenly Father—gifts we are to use wisely.

To give your children a feeling of communion with God and an awareness of God's mighty love, join them in outdoor projects that show God's bountiful nature and infinite love. Here are some ideas:

Plant a small vegetable garden. Let your child till the soil, plant each seed, and water the seeds until they sprout. Talk about God's plan for life to continue. Read Job 12:8.

Plant a flower garden. Using a packet of seeds or small starter plants, let your child feel the warm soil, smell the rich earth, and gently pack the seed or plant in the ground. Talk about God caring for us and protecting us. Read Psalm 150:6.

Go on a walk and pick a variety of wildflowers. Let your child pick these from along the roadside and then make them into an arrangement at home. Talk about how the flowers are all different, just like we are, and how God made each of us unique. Read Ecclesiastes 3:11.

Camp outside one night. Join your child to enjoy the wonder of nighttime—the pitch-black sky, the bright stars, the night sounds of crickets, birds, and other nocturnal animals. Talk about the majesty of God who planned our intricate world. Read Psalm 8:3–4,9.

Watch the sunrise. Have an early morning breakfast picnic outside and let your child see the rainbow of colors in the morning sky. Talk about new beginnings and how God lets us start new each day. Read Genesis 1:24.

Hang a bird feeder in your yard. Let your child keep the feeder filled with sunflower seeds or thistle. Watch the different birds come and notice how they grow. Talk about God's plan for us to grow in knowledge of Him through His Word. Read Job 12:7.

Collect fall leaves. Bring these home and press them with a warm iron between pieces of waxed paper. Display them on the refrigerator. Talk about the many colors of leaves and many races of people. Tell your child of God's love for all humankind. Read Genesis 8:22b.

Make snow angels on a cold day. Lie on the snow with your arms and legs straight. Open your arms and legs, then close them again. Talk about the wondrous beauty of God's earth and how we are an important part of this. Read 2 Corinthians 4:6b.

Collect trash from outside. Take a bag with you on the nature walk and collect any trash, bottles, or cans on the ground. Talk about being stewards of God's earth and how we are responsible for taking care of where we live. Read Psalm 145:2.

Share God's Love Each Day

Here are other ways to share God's love each day:

- Walk on the beach with bare feet and talk about the enormity of God's love for us.

- Have your child close his eyes and smell roses in the garden. Talk about the uniqueness of all God's children.

- Splash warm water over your child's hands while bathing him and talk about God giving us bodies to take care of.

- Stay after church as a family and quietly meditate on the stained glass windows. Pray together and thank God for the beauty of your family.

- Share some of the vegetables or flowers from your garden with a neighbor. Talk to your child about caring for others in God's world.

- Learn the names of the different trees in your yard or on your street. Talk about similarities and differences and how God has a special plan for each of us.

- Let your child take photographs of his nature hike—the colored leaves, the budding trees, the squirrels and caterpillars. Make an album entitled "All God's Kingdom," and let your child share this with grandparents.

- Get in the habit of purchasing a live Christmas tree and planting it after the holidays. Let your child care for this tree as he learns our responsibility to God's kingdom.

- Teach your child the words to a favorite hymn. Sing this together, then share the meaning of the words.

- Let your child listen to the sounds in a seashell. Help him to become aware of the many sounds in his life that God created.

- Read the story of Jesus with the children, found in Luke 10:13–16, and talk about how wonderful it is to be touched by Jesus' love.

SHARE GOD'S LOVE THROUGH PLAY

As you encourage your children to see God in daily experiences, don't forget the importance of meeting them "on common ground." From the toddler years through elementary school, play is their common ground. Arnold Gesell writes in his book, *The Child from Five to Ten*, "Children reveal themselves most transparently in their play life. They play not from outer compulsion, but from inner necessity."[4]

Parents often ask, "Have you ever tried to make an active two- or three-year-old sit still as you talk about God's love?" With our own children we often spent more time asking a young one to sit still than we did actually teaching. Even busy elementary-age children or energetic teens have difficulty paying attention for long periods of time when they would rather relax and *play* or feel free to create in their world.

As we encouraged play with our three children, we looked for "teachable moments" when we could share our love for God and His world. Play is important as the child learns the value of friendship. For example, by interacting with others, he discovers what cooperation is all about. He experiments with terms such as "mine," "yours," and "ours." He learns the benefits of give and take, sharing, and patience. And, through play, he learns to cope with frustrations that arise when situations don't go his way. What better way could the gospel message of *agape* love be taught to children than through this play experience?

Play Can Be Structured or Unstructured

Play can be both structured and unstructured as you encourage a daily awareness of God in your child's life. Structured play can include a puppet show, a biblical drama, or a role play. Unstructured play includes those moments when children sit under a tree and enjoy the beauty of nature, lie on a blanket and make imaginary cloud pictures, or interact with friends.

Children can learn about God's love as they reenact a Bible story, a parable, or a modern-day situation. A basket of scarves can magically take a child back 2,000 years. A small box becomes the manger where Jesus was born. A doll becomes that babe wrapped in swaddling clothes long ago in Bethlehem.

Provide Props for Make-Believe and Drama

Parents also can initiate meaningful play by providing props to boost creativity. Imaginative play is ongoing with children, and you can provide your child with the necessary tools. When our children were young, a dress-up box filled with old hats, jewelry, shirts, ties, shoes, and scarves gave them a daily opportunity to pretend and play make-believe. Through imaginative play a young child learns to express his likes and dislikes. He works through his problems and fears, and he finds an acceptable way to express his emotions.

Interact with Your Child

Play activities can enable your children to discover Christian values as they interact with others. Then, as the biblical message is taught, these precious values are reinforced and become ingrained in their developing minds.

How can you experience play with your children?

Play dramatic games together as you pretend to be Jesus' disciples helping other people or as you reenact the Christmas story. "Let's pretend" is a favorite expression for most young children, and dramatic games can be played after reading a Bible story so they can interpret the story personally.

Share in role plays as a family. This involves explaining a situation to the child, then asking her to get into a particular character's role. You can ask your child to interpret various feelings using body language, such as feeling sad, lonely, angry, loving, kind, or giving. Role play is especially effective for learning Christian responses to situations before they happen, such as "What would you do if a friend was being teased by other children?" or "What would you do if someone tried to take your sister's doll away?" For the older child, role play can deal with subjects like peer pressure and the Christian's response.

Suggest themes for structured and unstructured play. Themes like sharing, caring, helping, cooperating, taking turns, and brotherly love can help children learn how to be loving Christians.

Use creative arts and crafts for your child to express what he is feeling inside. Paints, crayons, colored chalk, and clay are just a few of the tools you can use at home as your child expresses his innermost feelings. On a rainy day, whip Ivory Snow and let your child "draw" pictures on your glass doors. An easy wipe cleans the doors later.

Provide opportunities each day for your child to sense problems and create solutions. This will help her relate favorite Bible stories to her life. Tell the story in words she can understand, then ask her to role play how this would relate to her life at home or at school.

Help the child form ideas for play based on specific themes. Depending on the Bible stories you are reading with your child, you may lead her in performing an impromptu drama depicting the Christmas story, a role play about the Good Samaritan, or a puppet show about David and Goliath.

ESTABLISH FAMILY RITUALS

As you work to strengthen your child's awareness of God in his daily life, launch out in faith and realize that no matter how difficult it is, you and your child can grow together in Christ's love. Taking time to establish rituals or traditions will increase this intimate bond between parent, child, and Jesus Christ—especially in our fast-paced society where family bonding is often diluted. Rituals for families offer a sense of identity in an impersonal era; they bring family members together, helping us to become rooted in the world. These roots ground us when we are faced with overwhelming problems in life.

When our son Rob was fifteen, he announced that he wanted no part of the usual family Christmas rituals anymore. "I'm too old for this. In fact, I can't decorate the tree this year. I've been invited to Jeff's house Friday night to sleep over," he told us. As much as we pleaded with him, he held his ground.

So on Friday, we shopped for the tree and decorated it without Rob. We had so much fun hanging the ornaments from previous years. We made our favorite spiced cider and helped Brittnye and Ashley decorate the sugar cookies. We took a picture of the four of us wearing our red stocking hats. It was truly a special time. When Rob came home Saturday, he looked at the decorated tree, the sugar cookies, and the family photo. Then he burst into tears. He was distraught that he had missed our special tradition and couldn't turn back time. From that time on, we have always made sure we are all together, if possible, for decorating at Christmas, or we save something the kids can do when they come home.

No matter the time or season of year, family traditions are ageless. They unite us with our past in a manner that offers comfort and reassurance. When an aging grandparent comments to the young child, "This Bible was mine when I was a young girl," all generations feel a warm sense of connectedness. Family traditions make us feel loved and help us to see God in daily living.

Your family's special ritual could be roasting marshmallows in the fireplace on cold winter nights, or making a favorite dinner together on Sunday evenings. It might be cooking out on Saturday evenings in the summer months, or going for early morning hikes in the spring and fall, or waiting for a good-morning kiss from Mom or Dad. Perhaps it is planting a spring garden together and harvesting it every Saturday as you experience nature and God's wonderment.

Whatever your family enjoys doing that is "uniquely theirs," *do it . . . again, and again, and again!* Only by repeating the ritual does it become a meaningful, shared experience. During this shared experience, you can talk about God's presence in your lives.

Start Traditions Today

What traditions can you begin with your family? Some easy ideas include:

- praying together before school

- eating dinner together every night

- reading a bedtime story with your child

- saying bedtime prayers with your child

- reading a Bible verse before a meal

- going for a short walk each evening

- going outside each morning for a breath of fresh air and prayer

- going out to breakfast before Sunday School and church

- having a family luncheon on Sundays

- going to Grandmom's house on Saturday afternoons

- calling the grandparents on Friday night, if they live far away

- writing "love notes" to each other and tucking them under the pillows

- having a family hug before leaving for the day

SHARE THE RESURRECTION STORY EVERY DAY

The following activities were written specifically for springtime as you share the Resurrection story with your child. You can adapt the activities to any season of the year, however, as you find ways *each day* to let your child experience God in his life.

Activities for Toddlers and Preschoolers

Go on an early morning hike with your child and marvel at the many changes. Incorporate all of your child's senses on the walk as you touch new leaves, smell flowers, see the blue sky, hear the birds chirping, and taste fresh fruit. Get on your hands and knees, and experience spring as your child does! What can he touch, smell, see, hear, and taste from his level?

Talk about God's creation. If it's springtime, talk about signs that winter is gone and spring is here, from the warmer weather to the longer days. Read Song of Solomon 2:11–12 out loud, and remind your child that new life during spring means that God intends for life to continue even after death.

Teach your child to anticipate new life in Jesus Christ. Read a book, such as *The Very Hungry Caterpillar*, to your child. Talk about the life cycle of the butterfly, and, in a way your child can understand, relate this transformation to God's plan for all creation as we grow from childhood into adulthood. Let your child reenact this transformation with a scarf as she huddles in a cocoon, then blossoms into a dancing, fluttering butterfly.

Let your child experience growth as you talk about personal physical growth. What changes has your preschooler undergone this year? Is he taller or wearing larger clothes? Living things start smaller and then grow larger. All of God's creatures experience growth as they develop into maturity.

If you are able, help your child collect and observe tadpoles as they go through their life cycle. Be sure to return the frogs to their environment! Share personal feelings about God's plan for all creation, and let your child know of God's love for the world.

Let your child know that Jesus was a child too. Using a children's Bible (as recommended in chap. 3), tell favorite stories about Jesus helping people. This will help your child see Jesus as a loving person who cares for others. Spend time singing your child's favorite songs about Jesus, such as "Jesus Loves Me." Remind your child that Jesus was a child just like them, then He grew into manhood.

Ask your child to do things Jesus did as a child—hop, skip, jump, clap hands, laugh. Join hands and do these activities with your child. Be sure to include Dad in these times so that your child will know that spiritual development and experiencing God's love are important to dads too!

Share God's love with your child as you read the Palm Sunday story from Matthew 21:1–11. Let your child role play Jesus' triumphant entry into Jerusalem as he waves his arms, symbolizing palm branches, and shouts "Hosanna." Emphasize to your child that people loved Jesus so much that they were singing and shouting as He rode by. Suggest ways your child can show love to family members and friends.

Activities for Elementary-School-Age Children

Tell your child why God through Jesus is important to you and discuss how your thoughts, words, actions, and relationships are affected by this love. Talk about how God makes Himself known through the Bible, through other Christians, and even through the transformation in nature during springtime. This celebration at Easter offers the perfect opportunity to tell your child about your personal relationship with God and what He means in your life.

Celebrate new life as you read the Resurrection story while out-of-doors during springtime. Being outside with God and nature makes the awareness of new life even more evident. Turn to Mark's account of the Easter story, and let your child read aloud: Mark 8:31; 9:31; 10:33–34; 14:27–28; and 16:1–16.

Reread the story of the Resurrection when the women went to the tomb and the stone was pulled away. What emotions did they experience? Role play the story and urge your child to capture with body movements the shock and excitement people felt when they realized that Jesus was alive.

Share God's love as you read the following situations to your child. Tell how the good news of the Resurrection can give strength as we share God's love with others. Tell how you would respond to this person, then ask your child to share his feelings:

- I am a student who is new to this city.

- I was not invited to the birthday party.

- I got a low grade on my paper.

- My sister fell off her bike.

- My dad has a cold.

- I struck out at my baseball game.

Let your child know that believing in God means that we must share His love with others when they are hurting or in need.

Encourage your child to live her faith each day as she leans on God's love. Have your child tell of ways she can let others see God's love that are "nonverbal" such as a hug, a kind deed, writing a note to a friend, or inviting a new child in school to sit with her. Encourage your child to follow through with these actions during the week.

Celebrate the Resurrection story with a traditional egg hunt. Explain that the egg is symbolic of new life, and all life is a gift from God. Emphasize that as Christians, we know that our lives will continue forever because of Jesus' Resurrection.

Remind your child that Jesus is alive today and wants to be a part of our lives. If he is ready, encourage him to ask Jesus into his heart this Easter with this prayer: "Lord Jesus, please forgive my sins and come into my life today. We thank you for your love in the world and for always being with us. Help us to share your love with others. Amen."

Activities for Older Children and Early Teens

Plan a family outing. Gather the entire family and head off for a lakeside picnic, dinner by a mountain stream, or lunch under the big tree in the yard. Go anywhere you can experience the beauty and newness of God's earth, anywhere the noise and busyness of daily life subsides.

Remind family members to bring their Bibles to your outing. Reading the Resurrection story, or any Bible story, while outdoors makes the awareness of God's love even more evident. An informal setting also helps self-conscious children and teens feel more comfortable as they tell of hopes and fears.

Turn to Mark's account of the Easter story and let your child or teen read aloud: Mark 8:31; 9:31; 10:33–34; 14:27–28; and 16:1–16. Mark's account of the Resurrection of Jesus is the briefest of all the Gospels. He focuses on the astonishment of the event and the profound effect it had on those who first visited the tomb. The first verses deal with Jesus' prediction of His impending death, while the last verses show how shocked those who first visited the tomb were.

Relive the Resurrection story. Ask your child or teen to think about the Resurrection and try to recapture what people on the scene must have thought and felt. Ask: If you were there grieving for your dear friend Jesus, what would you be thinking? How would you comfort yourself? When you approached the burial place, what would you think when the stone was rolled away? Would you be frightened, angry, or elated? Would you tell someone the glorious news that our friend, our Savior, was alive? Would people believe you?

Talk about sharing faith with others. Many times we have wonderful news of how God moves in our lives, but like the women at Jesus' tomb, we hesitate to share it. Even adults are timid in telling someone about their faith. Often we become so wrapped up in what we are going to say that we forget the needs of the other person. Jesus consistently listened with great care to the problems of others. As He drew out those who were sick or depressed, He ministered to their particular needs. He took each person seriously and responded to their specific concerns.

We can become "Easter people" as we talk about the contrast of the Crucifixion and the Resurrection with our children, as we experience the good and bad life has to offer, as we tell others of the love and new life Jesus can give. As you lead your children in the Bible study and suggested activities, share your own feelings and ideas. Talk about difficult times you've experienced when witnessing about Christ, and tell your children how you have launched out in faith and told others about Jesus Christ.

Join hands and lead your family members in a group prayer. Lift up the attributes and suggestions for witnessing that each person mentioned during the activities, and ask God to give your family strength as you are placed in situations where Christians must take a stand.

SPIRITUAL FOOD FOR THOUGHT

1. Talk to family members about the difficulties they may have in expressing their faith at home, school, work, and play. Talk about the other forces that may tear them down (peer pressure, unchurched friends, low self-esteem, lack of faith). Ask family members to identify the fears that may hold them back from talking about Christ to those around them such as "I don't know what to say," or "I don't know enough about the Bible," or "I'm afraid others might make fun of me or not like me anymore."

2. The best way to tell children how God moves in our lives is "through the eyes of our soul." Take time this week to go on an early morning walk with your child and talk about your personal belief in God. Relate your faith experience in simple terms. Talk about the emotions you felt when you realized that God, through Christ Jesus, was real to you.

3. Look for opportunities this week to talk about the majesty of God's kingdom. Be sure you make "spiritual moments," when you and your child take time to appreciate God's handiwork, such as feeling the rain, smelling the colorful flowers, identifying trees and plants on a nature hike. You may want to go outside at night and stargaze with your older child or teen and talk about being a part of God's plan.

4. Start a family ritual today that lets you appreciate the wonder of God's kingdom on earth. This may be an outdoor breakfast on a Saturday morning, a family prayer time before worship on Sunday, or a Bible study under a shade tree. Encourage your children to taste, smell, feel, see, and hear God's world, and talk about their experiences.

5. Look for play opportunities for younger children that allow expression of their senses. Provide a box of props, such as scarves and robes, and encourage them to act out biblical scenes, using the suggestions on pages 128 to 130. Older children or teens may wish to capture God's handiwork with a camera. Purchase a photo album for them to keep a visual record of what they experience.

Seven

Nurture Christian Values

When our son Rob was in fifth grade, we took him to a week-long church camp. Upon arrival, we had to register him, and we spent a long time filling out the required forms. As we handed the forms and a handful of bills over to the camp registrar and introduced Rob to his counselors, Ashley tugged on our shirts. With tears in her eyes she said, "Please, Mommy and Daddy, please don't sell Robbie!"

Rob knew he wasn't being sold, and we comforted his younger sister. Yet Ashley expressed a great need of children: to know that they have an important place in the world—in their homes. This, of course, is the great tragedy of the breakup of families today. Each of us needs to know that something in our lives is stable and secure. Home is where our children learn trust and confidence; and home is where we learn such values as honesty, courage, enthusiasm, service, faith, and love.

One night years ago we tucked Brittnye and Ashley into bed with all the necessary ritual, only to be called back into their room several times. Finally, after hearing a bloodcurdling scream, we rushed to their room and demanded to know what the problem was this time.

"I got shocked by that lamp!" Ashley cried.

"You got shocked? How in the world did you do that?" Bob shouted.

"I wanted to see if the lamp was really working, so I took the lightbulb out and stuck my finger in the hole," she whimpered.

Perhaps what Ashley really wanted to know is that she mattered in her home and that she could trust her parents to protect her. Children—all children—have a tremendous need to be aware of their own significance. Actually, we all have that need, although most of us satisfy it in ways other than sticking our fingers into electrical sockets.

Everyone's talking about "values" today. These principles that we strive to live by reflect an ideal moral standard, and not only benefit individuals and families, but also society as a whole. Close family relationships teach values as the family provides our first understanding of traditional ethics and personal standards.

With responsible training at home, parents can enable their child to learn how to make moral decisions, to distinguish right from wrong, and to exhibit ethical behavior. Psychologists such as Lawrence Kohlberg believe that moral behavior is predicted by the growth stage a child is in. Kohlberg has identified developmental stages of children as they mature into adolescence, then adulthood. According to Kohlberg, a child may try to avoid punishment from ages two to six, do "trade-offs" with others ("If you'll be nice, I'll be nice") from ages six to ten, believe fully in law and order from ages eleven to fifteen, and begin to understand democracy and conscience at fourteen years on up.[1] While this concept of moral development in stages is accepted by many, we feel it greatly downplays the role spirituality and faith play in a child's ability to discern right from wrong.

Other psychologists concur that in children the seeds of morality are emotional, not intellectual. Such traits as empathy and guilt—observable in the very young—represent the beginning of what later will become a conscience. Even newborns respond to signs of distress in others. In a hospital nursery, for example, a bout of crying by one infant will trigger wailing all around. Research on children's attachment to their mothers shows that the babies who are most secure (and whose mothers are most responsive to their needs) later turn out to be leaders in school—self-directed and eager to learn. They also are the most likely to absorb parental values.[2]

THE FAMILY IS A TESTING GROUND

Within the nest of this accepting group of people called the family, a child can experiment with all sorts of rebellious behavior, testing to see what will be approved and what won't. Even though your home teaches the love of Christ, chances are that, as your child passes into the stormy times of adolescence, she will be tempted to "test the waters" in various ways. She may try cheating on tests at school, or she may begin to use trendy slang and wear unsuitable outfits to school. The older child or young teen may rebel against going to church or try to get out of family outings. Sooner or later, your child will want to see if Mom and Dad are really serious about this "values stuff."

Parents must be serious about values. You are the single most important influence on your children. Parents who spend time daily talking about morals and personal standards to live by will be rewarded with a child who will go into the world with strong character and charity toward others. Good families know that part of their role is to free their members when the time comes to function as healthy, responsible adults. Most parents rejoice when their children can stand on their own, think for themselves, and make good decisions based on common sense and experience.[3]

In Ephesians 6:4, Paul warns Christian parents: "Don't keep on scolding and nagging your children, making them angry and resentful. Rather, bring them up with the loving discipline the Lord himself approves, with suggestions and godly advice."

Parenting is about relationships—loving relationships. In order to teach Christian values in your home, you must spend time with your child and get to know him. Did you know you are the "gatekeeper" of your family? One of your main tasks is to create a warm, caring home environment where each child can feel loved and affirmed.

Picture a gatekeeper in biblical times keeping track of all the sheep, large and small, young and old, as they graze in the nearby pastures. If one sheep becomes lost or hurt along the way, the shepherd leaves the flock to find and comfort that single sheep.

Shepherds develop a special relationship with their sheep because of the amount of time spent together. In John 10:3, Jesus says, "The sheep hear his voice, and he calls his own sheep by name and leads them out" (RSV).

In our increasingly urban culture, it's easy to miss the force of this image. In Jesus' day, a shepherd would know every sheep in the flock. He would know each sheep's habits and traits. He would be able to predict the sheep's behavior under any condition or set of circumstances. This is the same type of closeness a parent must have with her child if Christian values are to be taught.

You can develop special relationships in your family as you plan opportunities each day to spend time with each child. A trip out to lunch for just the two of you, a leisurely walk around the block, or doing a project together can give you new insight into the thoughts and concerns of your developing child.

But You Live in the "Dark Ages"

But what about the teen years? What is it about this stage that makes teaching personal standards difficult? As parents of three teens, we find that perhaps the most difficult stumbling block confronting us is the generation gap. Teens are fighting hard to break the apron strings as they seek independence, and that creates friction even in the most loving homes.

In our family, at one time or another, we have had three "mini-adults" look us straight in the eyes and matter-of-factly say, "Well, Mom, don't forget that those were the 'dark ages' when you were a teen-ager," or, "Face it, Dad. You're just not with it anymore." How do we respond? We stand strong! No matter how offensive these words are, parents must remain strong with the highest morals and values as this age group tests their limits.

Trust and Confidence

Trust and confidence are primary building blocks of the home. As you teach your child Christian values, it's vital that you have the trust of your children.

A story is told about a stuntman who pulled a tightrope across the Niagara Falls and announced he was going to walk across and back. A large crowd gathered for the event. He started walking and made it to the other side, and the crowd applauded. Then he attempted to walk back; he made it again, and everyone applauded even louder. People who said that it couldn't be done suddenly became believers. Then he took a wheelbarrow and walked the wheelbarrow across. By this time, *everyone* was a believer. Then he asked, "Now, before I take the wheelbarrow back once more, I'm going to ask for a volunteer. Who will ride in the wheelbarrow?" Applauding believers suddenly drew back! Who would go with this madman? Yet one young child came forward and climbed into the wheelbarrow. "Of course the little girl would trust him," a bystander observed correctly. "He is her father."

Your children should trust you just as that child trusted her father. Yet a recent study reported that *more than half of all American teenagers don't have anyone they trust and want to be like.* This poll revealed that many teens have no heroes at all.

Our children are searching for heroes, someone they can model their lives after, and parents should provide that model.

Paul teaches us to "pattern your lives after mine and notice who else lives up to my example" (Phil. 3:17). To our children, we are like stationary planets, and they are the tiny satellites revolving around us. Everything we do or say as parents will be mimicked by them. If we pray each day, they will learn to do the same. If they see us reading the Bible every morning, they will know it is important to us. If we go together to Sunday School and church each week, we will help them develop a habit they will take into adulthood. Can your children trust you to leave them a spiritual legacy?

SELF-ESTEEM STARTS AT HOME

To stand strong for the high personal standards you teach at home, your child must feel secure with positive self-esteem. Self-esteem is a child's feeling about himself and the basis of his respect for self and others.

Building a child's self-esteem begins when he is in the womb. The way we touch, speak to, and meet the needs of that tiny infant will determine how he will feel about himself. Children with high self-esteem are less likely to abuse drugs and alcohol, have early sexual experiences, or follow the crowd. They have a strong inner confidence that allows them to stand strong for the personal standards they believe in.

You can boost your child's self-concept through many daily activities. Children with a positive self-concept need someone—a parent—who believes in them unconditionally, like God believes in us. They need adults who nurture them with praise, hugs, and discipline; who comfort them when they fail; and who nudge them out the door to try again and again.

The ability to nurture is not an option. It's essential—if you want to rear healthy children. In essence, nurturing is the spiritual quality of parenthood, the intangible element that separates the good from the bad and the adequate from the inadequate. It is the instinct to comfort your child when she is sick, to soothe her when she is frightened. Parents who nurture best do a lot of touching and kissing; and while their children may feign embarrassment, these kids are the ones who are the most secure—the learners, the leaders.[4]

WHAT VALUES MUST WE TEACH?

Children will model their lives after their parents. The child who learns at home that it's wrong to hit others or take things that aren't his will go into the world—at school or play—and live this behavior. Likewise, a child who learns at home that calling people names, disrespecting authority, and lying are not acceptable will act responsibly in public places. From the family, children learn to care for the needy, to show compassion when someone is hurting, and to reach out in love to those who need to know Jesus Christ.

Christian values transcend the "family values" you hear about from the media. Anyone can display "family values" by being fair, kind, and decent. Yet God calls Christians to a higher level of decency. He challenges us to follow Jesus Christ and pattern our lives after His actions, our words after His. Jesus' ministry was one of making choices. As He confronted people in different situations, He encouraged them to make firm commitments and decisions about their life—to choose between good and evil. The uniqueness of the New Testament lies in this new freedom that Jesus taught, freeing us from the bondage of the Old Testament law.

As Christians, God calls us to be obedient in the midst of freedom. By taking action and making moral choices, we will model responsibility to our developing children as we teach the following.

Teach *Agape* Love

Throughout the Bible, the message of *love* is spoken of more than 500 times; it is a most powerful word! In 1 Corinthians 13,

Paul describes Christian love as an active and vital force. The type of perfect love Paul teaches stems from God: "God's love has been poured into our hearts through the Holy Spirit which has been given to us" (Rom. 5:5, RSV). This Christian love is very different from the "love" being trumpeted by television, magazines, and movies. *Philio* (friendship) and *eros* (erotic desire) can begin a love relationship, but these types of love can die—friends part; and beauty or sexual appeal diminish. Yet Paul tells us about *agape* love, a self-giving charity filled with compassion and empathy. This type of love seeks what is best for others, then sets out with unconditional caring to meet those needs. It continues to care and show compassion for the other—even when the person loved is broken, facing problems, ill, or acts unlovely. *Agape* love never changes. This is the love we are to teach our children.

Teach Empathy

To have empathy means to be sensitive to the needs of others, and having empathy for your child involves seeking the best for him. A friend said, "When my son asked to go away last summer to be a counselor at a New England resort, I immediately said no. Then, after thinking about it for a few days, I realized that he needed time away from us. He was old enough and mature enough to handle this experience, and I wanted him to know what it's like to be on your own."

Teaching empathy and living empathetically are two different things. Anyone can tell a child that it's good to care for others and that the Golden Rule (do unto others as you would have them do unto you) is a proper guideline for living. Yet Christians must take this teaching one step further: We must insist on moral behavior and kindness in our homes.

We can remind children to treat others with compassion, but when we see them acting contrary to this, we must call them to task. For example, if your child calls his brother a name, immediately ask, "How would you feel if he said that to you?" If your child tells you that he doesn't want to go to Grandma's on Sunday afternoon, help him become sensitive to others by asking, "How would you feel if we planned on Grandma coming to our home and she backed out?" Or, if your child tells you kids were making fun of the new girl at school and he sat by her at lunch to make her feel good, praise him!

Let your child know through simple conversation that you are human and have feelings, just like she does. Tell her what God is doing in your own life, and help her to see your Christian standards by discussing the priorities in your life. Help her to understand why you took supper to the neighbors' house when there was a death in the family, why you did the laundry for an ill friend, why you volunteer to build houses for the needy, why you donate canned goods for Thanksgiving and Christmas baskets. Talk to her about the importance of family—caring for elderly relatives and keeping in touch with members who live far away.

When our children learn to love others as they love themselves, they are truly following the greatest commandment of all: "Love the Lord your God with all your heart, soul, and mind. . . . Love your neighbor as much as you love yourself" (Matt. 22:37–38).

Teach Right from Wrong

As parents, we are the most important role models our children have, and we can lead the way to moral behavior in the home. The old adage, "Do as I say, not as I do," *does not work* with children. Children look to us for direction and learn by our example, so we must try to practice what we preach and be consistent in our behavior.

We can seize the opportunities every day to get our message across—whether it's teaching respect for the property of others or always telling the truth. We can explain the concepts of cause and effect and truth and consequence by using examples from news events to reinforce our point. We should never be afraid to discuss with our children the moral shortcomings of our society.[5]

Children must learn to distinguish between right and wrong as they learn Christian values at home. And parents have to teach them. The idea that children just randomly turn out good or bad and should be free to determine their own moral course is a relatively new (and foolish) idea. *No parent can control everything a child does, but every parent has a responsibility before God for how his or her children are reared.*

Most children appreciate knowing the boundaries of behavior. In fact, many studies confirm that children reared by "authoritative" parents are more likely to be self-reliant, self-controlled, and contented. Thomas Lickona, professor of education at the State University of New York and author of *Raising Good Children,* says that adolescents most likely to follow their consciences rather than give in to peer pressure are those who grew up in "authoritative" homes, where rules are firm but clearly explained and justified— as opposed to "authoritarian" homes, where rules are laid down without explanation, or "permissive" homes.[6]

Teach the Ten Commandments

While we are giving rules to our children, we cannot forget the importance of teaching them the Ten Commandments. From the covenant relationship God established with Israel, Moses received a set of principles to live by, which we know as the Ten Commandments. These rules offer strength to believers, telling us the distinct difference between right and wrong.

The first four deal with our relationship to our Creator:

"I am the Lord your God, who brought you out of the land of Egypt, out of the house of bondage. You shall have no other gods before me. You shall not make for yourself a graven image. . . . You shall not take the name of the Lord your God in vain. . . . Observe the Sabbath day, to keep it holy" (Deut. 5:6–12, RSV).

The remaining six commandments deal with our relationship to others:

"Honor your father and your mother. . . . You shall not kill. Neither shall you commit adultery. Neither shall you steal. Neither shall you bear false witness against your neighbor. Neither shall you covet" (Deut. 5:16–21, RSV).

The Ten Commandments are rules of human conduct and eternal guiding principles that every child should know and understand.

Teach Gratitude

When we reflect back on our childhood years, we can both honestly say that giving thanks seldom occupied our thoughts. Like most kids, we were so wrapped up with the "real" business of life—ourselves, our friends, our school activities—that offering thanks to God or others wasn't on our mind. Yet through the years we have learned that giving thanks is an essential part of our faith—even for children and teens. When we take time regularly to realize our blessings and acknowledge God's gifts, we can reach out with His love to others.

PRACTICES FOR PARENTS

Along with teaching our children values, we also have a duty to hold fast to personal standards as we represent security to our children. What should we practice to be strong as a parent?

Practice Saying *No*

Most people have a difficult time saying *no*. Sometimes we get hooked into frustrating situations simply because we *just can't refuse*. Part of this inability to say *no* stems from our fear of offending others. We also hesitate in saying *no* because we don't want to be thought "insensitive."

Yet is it always caring to say *yes* to your child if you know the consequences will be negative? Is it sensitive to say *yes* if you know your child will be hurt in the long run? Saying *yes* to all the requests your child makes daily not only puts you in a weak position, but also retards her moral development. Don't be afraid to say *no* if you feel your child is injuring her integrity or character.

Practice the Healing Power of Touch

We have been conditioned to be a "hands-off" society. Yet a pat on the shoulder, a hug, or a loving back rub often pack the same power as saying, "I love you."

Ralph Waldo Emerson said, "I never like the giving of the hand, unless the body accompanies it." Jesus showed this love especially to children as He "took them in his arms and blessed them, laying his hands upon them" (Mark 10:16, RSV). In the Scriptures, touch played an important part in the bestowing of a family blessing.

Touch also has a magnificent healing property. One recent study reported that an estimated 30,000 North American nurses now employ therapeutic touch—an updated, nonreligious version of the biblical laying on of hands, based on the notion of a human energy field. Some studies have reported that the benefits of massage or touch include heightened alertness, relief from depression and anxiety, an increase in the number of natural "killer cells" in the immune system, lower levels of the stress hormone cortisol, and reduced difficulty in getting to sleep.

How often do you hug your child? Your touch may be the security she longs for.

Practice Forgiveness

Forgiveness is a gift from God. We have been forgiven, and thus we are able to forgive others. Jesus told a parable about a man who owed his king 10,000 talents. We are told that this was an amount equivalent to fifteen years of wages to a laborer in that day. The king forgave the man his debt. This man, however, had an acquaintance who owed him 100 denari—about a single day's wages. The man who had his enormous debt discharged by the king would not forgive the tiny debt owed him by the neighbor.

He had the man thrown in jail (Matt. 23:18–35). He was forgiven a fortune, yet he refused to forgive a trifle. The contrast is striking.

Of course, Jesus is talking about you and me. We have been forgiven by God; we are sinners saved by grace. That is what the cross of Calvary is all about—the forgiveness of an enormous debt that we have received by God's grace!

Remember the saying, "Love means never having to say you're sorry"? Actually, real love frequently says, "I'm sorry." An apology, along with God's forgiveness, is vital in building deep relationships. You communicate to your child, "I respect you and your feelings," when you admit being wrong. Showing humility toward our children while asking for their forgiveness is not easy, but laying aside pride is essential to any loving relationship (see Phil. 2: 1–9).

How can you teach forgiveness in your home?

Openly say, "I'm sorry." The best way to admit that you were wrong is to be genuine and up front with your child, especially if you came down hard on him and now feel remorse.

Write a love note. A sincere, written apology can express your innermost feelings and affirm your love for him. This note should follow a verbal apology—not precede it.

Talk with your child on "common ground." Go out for a treat alone with your child. Choose his favorite—an ice cream cone or hamburger and fries. Sometimes it's easier to talk with our children when we're on equal turf instead of at home where the parent "rules."

Talk with your child about how much God has forgiven us and how we are to forgive others (read Matt. 18:21–34). Tell of a time when someone wronged you and the difficulty you had in offering forgiveness. Encourage your child to share his feelings.

Admit you are human too. Parents are often required to know all the right answers, and that's a lot of pressure! Admit to your child that you are doing the best you can as a parent. Explain your point of view, then humbly say, "I'm sorry."

Join hands and pray together. Ask God to help mend your parent-child relationship and give you a more Christlike attitude as parent.

TRY "TABLE TALKS"

Mounting evidence reveals that the one thing families lack today is *together time.* Family meals took a priority in our home as our children grew up. We have found that as moms, dads, and children come together for food and fellowship, affirmation and acceptance bloom.

Make certain that your family members set aside time to eat together. You can use this time to share the following activities with all members as you engage in Table Talk. This is a family discussion that lasts just a few minutes each evening, enabling your child or teen to get in touch with the values and high standards you are trying to teach.

Discover your strengths. At the dinner table, ask members to tell their five greatest strengths. Then, ask them to tell two strengths of each member around the table. For example, eleven-year-old Erica might say her greatest strengths are caring, study habits, being a good friend, patience, and neatness. She might add that her eight-year-old brother's strengths are being funny and being a good listener, and Mom's strengths are keeping fit and teaching school.

Take time to share these strengths and enjoy the special gifts in your family. Join hands and close with a simple prayer, thanking God for each person.

Create a thankful acronym. After dinner, have each family member write the word "thankfulness" down the side of a piece of the paper. During Table Talk, ask members to write something they are thankful for that starts with each letter of the word, then share the results. This can be adapted for younger children by asking them to tell things they are thankful for.

For example, nine-year-old Pete may write:

Teachers
Having fun with friends
A in Reading
New puppy
Kind parents, sometimes
Food
Uniforms for baseball
Love
Nice teachers
Everybody in my family
Singing in the junior choir
Starting guitar lessons

Create a thankful mural. Read Luke 17:11–19 to your children. This is a story about a man who returned to Jesus to say thanks after being healed. Have your child draw pictures of himself saying thank you to Jesus for things He has done for him.[7] This is a perfect activity for the entire family—even toddlers love to scribble on paper. Hang the mural in your kitchen over the breakfast table and celebrate your many blessings.

Talk about right and wrong. Have older children and teens make two lists on a sheet of paper. On one list, ask them to write down behaviors they know are right; on the other list, ask them to write down behaviors they know are wrong. Talk about why certain behaviors are acceptable and others are not. How does our Christian faith influence our behaviors? Have younger children tell you right and wrong behaviors. Affirm their developing sense of morality and values.

Focus on special people. So many people help to make us who we are. While our parents are most important in establishing our moral code, there are Sunday School teachers, preschool teachers, ministers, neighbors, grandparents, aunts, uncles, and more who contribute to our lives. Do some Table Talk and focus on special people from the past. Give your children or teenagers a piece of paper and a pencil after dinner tonight. During Table Talk ask them to list special people through the years who have touched their life. This may include their first-grade teacher, a baseball coach, a next-door neighbor, the minister, and grandparents. Provide them with stationery and stamps, and encourage them to write a simple letter to these people, thanking them for affirmation and training during the early years. Be sure to include a photograph and return address. Younger children can draw a picture and Mom or Dad can write a thank-you note.

Make a family statement. During Table Talk, establish personal standards that your family believes in, and write them on paper. Your family statement may include, "We believe in honesty. We believe in morality. We believe in not cheating or stealing. We believe in not using alcohol and illegal drugs." Before you begin your meal each night, take a minute and read this list. Close with a prayer to God as you offer thanks to Him for the strength of your family members to abstain from a secular society's ways.

Exchange your thanks. Give each family member a sheet of paper and pencil after dinner. During Table Talk ask them to write their name at the top of the page, then pass this around the table until they each have someone else's paper. Have each person write what they would be thankful for if they were the person whose name is on the paper. For example, if twelve-year-old John gets seven-year-old Missy's paper, he might write, "Missy is thankful for good grades, her new doll, piano lessons, and especially for a remarkable older brother." If Missy gets Dad's paper, she might write: "Dad is thankful for his job, playing golf, and a sweet daughter—Missy!" Share these papers when everyone is through, and enjoy the many gifts your family has. Adapt this for younger children by talking about special gifts of those in your family.

Find the good in the bad. Do some Table Talk with family members about a time when they had troubles. This may have been when your child did poorly on a test, struck out during the baseball finals, or lost his reading book. Encourage him to find something positive to be thankful for—though life seemed bleak at that time. For example, if ten-year-old Jacob got a *C* on his reading test last week, although it may have been a down time, he can be thankful for learning that he needs to study harder to succeed. If nine-year-old Elizabeth struck out on her softball team, she can be thankful for the many friends on the team and should be encouraged to try again next time. Talk about giving thanks to God for everything life offers, and share how you have learned to see God in the midst of adversity.

WHEN VALUES ARE MORE THAN WORDS

Believing in Jesus Christ calls for a personal response from each of us. As you share values with your child, it is important that you talk about putting these words into action. God calls for us to respond to Him with lives marked by change. When we show obedience to Him and practice justice and mercy toward others, we are responding in a Christlike manner. How can your child respond with Christian values? She can:

- stand up for a friend who is being treated unfairly

- refuse to gossip

- set the record straight when falsehoods are spoken

- forgive someone who has offended you or hurt you

- meet the needs of someone in your class or neighborhood

- spend time in Bible study and prayer

- change a lifestyle that doesn't fit God's will for your life[8]

TEACH YOUR CHILDREN WELL

Many would agree that Christian parents have a lot of catching up to do as the secular world crashes into our homes and tries to destroy our personal standards. Because we all need a code to live by, parents must be the first teachers of the child. We can no longer leave the moral and ethical development of our children up to the schools or society. Even the church can fail us where morals and Christian values are concerned. As you encourage spiritual development with your child, realize that *you are the most important role model in her life.* How you act, react, speak, and make choices in your everyday life will be observed by her and acted out in her own life. Remember, *now* is the time to reassume your responsibility to teach and live Christian values in your family.

FAMILY TIME—MAKING CHOICES

Use the following family time activity to reinforce the values that are dear to you. Give your child a sheet of paper and ask him to write down behaviors in his life that are right and behaviors that are wrong. A younger child may tell you what is right or wrong instead of writing this. For example:

Right	**Wrong**
obeying my parents	talking back
respecting my teacher	making fun of friends
doing my own homework	cheating on tests
loving my sister and brother	hurting people

Talk with your child about this list and ask, "How do you know what is right and what is wrong?" Let him know that when God is in our life, He gives us direction for making the right choices. If your child is still learning to make responsible decisions, you can assist him in understanding the process with the following approach.

Offer choices. Depending on the child's maturity, *start with simple choices* that affect his daily life. For example, ask: "Do you want peanut butter or cheese on your sandwich?" or "Do you want to wear your sweater or sweatshirt today?" As your child learns to make a reasonable choice and live with the result, you can *add more complex choices,* asking: "Do you want to buy the hot lunch, buy a sandwich, or take your lunch box today?" or "Do you want to invite Sammy over today, work on your new clubhouse, or play your video game?"

Teach him to consider the alternatives. Each time your child makes a choice, talk about the alternatives by asking: "Why did you choose that? Is there another choice that would also work?"

Discuss the consequences. Every action your child takes has a reaction, either good or bad. Help your child think through the pros and cons of his choices by questioning: "How will that help you? hurt you? Is it respectful to all, including family and friends? Will it hurt anyone else? Do you feel comfortable with this?"

Evaluate the decision. Through evaluation your child can grow in wisdom even when his choice did not work out. Ask: "Would you make the same choice next time? Why? Why not? What would you do the same? differently? What did you learn from this?"

During family time, use the following outline to teach your child creative problem solving. Present a problem, then let him brainstorm all possible alternatives—even silly ones! Discuss responsible decision making and making wise choices.

1. Present the problem.

2. Discuss the alternatives. What other options are there?

3. Think about the consequences. List pros and cons of each.

4. Evaluate the choice made. Did it work? Why? Why not?

SPIRITUAL FOOD FOR THOUGHT

1. What are some of your family's values and personal standards? How are you conveying or modeling these to your children?

2. Explain some differences you have had with your child or teen over your family's values or rules. Read Ephesians 6:4 and share the meaning this has in your life for sharing values.

3. Take time this week to go over your family's standards with your children. Have your children write these down on a sheet of paper and post these for all to see.

4. Write down the times your child shows empathy or tells about being compassionate this week. Compliment him for doing this, and take note of his reaction to your affirmation.

5. Look for the "God" in your child. If your child is in a rebellious stage, it may be difficult to see her good qualities, but make an effort to find these and praise her openly. Does your belief in her make a difference in how she treats others?

Eight

Stand Strong against the Odds

Ours was a pristine, unblemished, please-and-thank-you family until the first day of preschool, when young Rob came home with a big grin pasted across his face and a new vocabulary: a series of four-letter words that would make a sailor blush. Rob was proud of his new language, for he realized that when he said one of these expletives, everyone—children and adults—would look his way. Negative attention beats no attention at all, and suddenly the world was focusing on him. "Everyone, including the teacher, looks right at me when I use these words," he said proudly.

Yet his moment of stardom faded fast. He immediately learned that if these words were used—anywhere—he would suffer the painful consequences of timeout, no cartoons, or, even worse, no friends after school.

Perhaps you've been there, and know that it isn't easy being a Christian parent in today's world. Not only are we hit with words unlike those we use at home, but our children confront opposing values as soon as they leave us—even for preschool. We have found that one of the most difficult tasks for Christian parents is to block worldly influences from affecting our children and our family.

Christians are bombarded daily with issues and demands that tug at the very core of our beliefs. As we encourage spiritual development with our children, how do we handle outside influences on the family?

Overwhelmed by potentially negative influences, many parents shield their children against the perils of the world in order to keep them safe. Yet the truth is that our children are going to learn about the world's value system. We can't shelter them forever, nor should we. What we can do is watch for teachable moments to explain to our children valuable lessons about life, God, family, and being a Christian in a pluralistic world today.[1]

Opposing Values Have Always Existed

Since the beginning, humans have faced obstacles and resistance in the world. Paul tells us, "[You are] engaged in the same conflict which you saw and now hear to be mine" (Phil. 1:30, RSV). We are not the first followers of Christ to face a society with opposing values! But remember that the only real enemies we have are *Satan, the world that ignores Christ,* and the *flesh.* All believers are part of a godly team contending for the gospel, and the challenge is that *we must stand together to function as one team.*

In a secular society, people will always oppose what and who you are. Yet most do not deliberately set out to destroy our faith. Rather, they are wrestling with their own sin—feeling guilt and shame, while not wanting to stop sinning. Still, we can stand strong against opposing forces by enjoying Christ's blessings: "If there is any encouragement in Christ, if any incentive of love, if any fellowship, any participation in the Spirit, affection and sympathy, be of the same mind" (Phil. 2:1–2, RSV).[2]

God has provided for humankind a set of strict values and standards to follow. As your child matures, he will begin to see certain realities in the world.

- There is a right and wrong to everything.

- Not all people do what is fair and right.

- Some people take advantage of others whenever possible.

- There are good and bad people.

- Not everyone is loving and kind.

- Some people will be unfair and unkind for almost any reason.

- Not all people go to Sunday School and church.

- Many people use profane language and speak ungodly thoughts.

- Pushing and shoving is a way of life for many people.[3]

While these truths will certainly become apparent to our children as they grow up, we can give them some tools to cope with opposing influences so the foundation of their Christian faith is not weakened.

BE IN THE WORLD, NOT OF THE WORLD

Our Lord will provide all that we need for emotional health as Christians, as we are called to *live in the world, but not be of the world*. This means that we can experience an abundant life right where we are without giving into society's demands. While this does not mean that we are to isolate ourselves in Christian communes, we do need to take seriously the challenge to be role models for Christ and live as He taught.

We are a people who belong to God, and self-control and self-discipline are essential qualities for Christians facing a hostile society. In 1 Peter 1:13, we read: "Prepare your minds for action; discipline yourselves." This self-control is vital, especially as Christians face the following challenges in a secular world:

- school and extracurricular activities that conflict with family times

- contradicting and secular values

- television shows, movies, and videos with sexual overtones and discriminate against minorities and women

- adult teachers and leaders whose morals differ drastically from those taught at home

- friends whose values and morals are in conflict to yours

- opinions given in classrooms and groups that are inconsistent with a Christian's beliefs

- church leaders who may not be answering God's call

- the lure of having social status

EVEN CHRISTIANS ARE DIVERSE

Diversity among people is nothing new. Not only are people in the world different, but Christians within the church have varying opinions, depending on their background, education, and environment. Even in the earliest days of the church, people experienced differences in viewpoints and convictions. Yet Paul affirmed the unity of Christians in Romans 12:5: "We, though many, are one body in Christ" (RSV).

Perhaps the most frequent expression we have heard during the teenage years is, "But everybody else gets to," or "Joe's Mom or Sally's Dad lets them do it." How do we respond? There is only one answer: *We aren't everyone else, and in our family we do not do that.* This brings about the perfect opportunity to explain your family's values and standards to your children. Tell them why your family doesn't go to certain movies or watch questionable television shows. Tell them why your family does not use "profanity" or wear suggestive clothes. Most importantly, affirm what is right and good about your family and the personal standards you have chosen to follow. Read to them from the Bible and let them see the verses you select that challenge Christians to decency, high morals, and Christlike values and behavior.

The world is very alluring to most people. As our children grow up, they will be tempted to succumb to worldly standards, such as premarital sex or gratification with alcohol or drugs. Often these pressures overwhelm questioning teens, and they struggle to stand firm in their beliefs.

C. S. Lewis reminds us that *only good men are bothered by temptation.* Bad men don't consider it temptation because they always succumb to it! In these moments of temptation, we must teach our children to deal with opposition head-on. While they cannot ignore the temptation or the peer who is luring them into worldly behavior, they can deal with it by saying "No!" or confronting the person. Dealing with the potential sin may be difficult, but the consequences of falling into sin are far worse.

Prayer is very effective in the fight against opposing forces or temptation. In the Lord's Prayer, Jesus asked God to "lead us not into temptation" (Luke 11:4, RSV). Remember that God does not tempt us (see James 1:13), but He does guide our lives. Jesus prayed that God would lead Him and His disciples away from temptation and toward obedience, and our children can learn to do the same.[4]

WHAT MUST WE DO TO STAND STRONG?

Teach your child that the cost of being a Christian in a secular world is high, but God demands unconditional surrender to His will. He asks us to do things that take a great deal of effort and that may be painful. Especially when saying no to hostile forces, children need to understand that standing strong is what Christians must do—even when it's tough.

Stand Firm for Personal Standards

Because we live in a free and diverse society where everyone can "speak their mind," our children face many challenges to their faith at school, work, and play. With increasing technological advances, not even your home is sacred; television, radio, magazines, newspapers, and even your home computer can introduce a child to a world of opposing values. Knowing this, you must teach your children ways to handle these outside influences.

Encourage Openness with Your Child

First, *talk* about the opposing force, whether it's a television show that has sexual overtones, a friend's parent who uses profane language, a teacher who calls students inappropraite names, or school rules you disagree with. Parents can give strength and reassurance as children share their feelings of resentment and anger. Empathy and caring can take place as these concerns and feelings are expressed. Use such times to clarify your family's rules and values, and explain why they are significant to your family. Many families never talk about *why* they believe in what they do until someone challenges them.

Know When to Draw the Line

One of the most important tools for dealing with such situations is knowing when to draw the line. Parents must talk about their values and goals in order for change to take place. As the leaders in the home, we have to decide when to draw the line as outside influences interrupt family time, interfere with family values, or influence our children in a negative manner.

Whatever the outside influence is, remember: *You set the rules and limits for your children, not school or society.*

Set Limits on the Media

Christian values not only aren't reinforced by the media in our culture, they are attacked—making it impossible at times to encourage spirituality in the home. Many children spend more time listening to television than their parents or teachers. It's easy to allow children to keep company with the television, but the tube is often another stumbling block in a child's maturation and spiritual development.

Develop Family Standards

The media—including television, movies, videos, magazines, and newspapers—are some of the greatest opposing influences in Christian homes. As you gain control of their influence in your home, develop some family standards. Read the following questions to your children, then set appropriate limits for your family. Children make wiser decisions if they know the rules. We ask these questions in our family; they can be modified to apply to any form of media.

1. Is the program or movie something your child would choose to watch, or is it just blaring noise?

2. How much time has your child spent watching TV (or videos) today? this week?

3. If your child weren't watching TV or videos, would she be engaged in a more productive activity, such as exercise, reading, or interacting with family and friends?

4. Does the show or magazine promote the Christian values you believe in and are teaching your child?

5. Does the program or movie portray violence or graphic sexual activities? Does it show different races of people in a negative light?

6. Is the show something your child would choose to watch, or is it just a habit at this time of day?

7. Is there a program on public television that might be educational for the child?

8. Is your child old enough to understand that the program is make-believe?

9. Is the program or movie uplifting, educational, or entertaining, or does it make you depressed and dull?

10. Does the show promote your Christian family values?

11. Are slang terms or offensive language used on the show something that might be picked up by your child?

HOW CAN WE CONTINUE LIVING IN THE WORLD?

Resisting outside influences is difficult, especially when others follow the crowd. Your child may feel his world has fallen in when you say no to an activity or questionable influence. Yet God gives strength to begin anew. Fellowship and communication within the family are vital; strength comes from this tightknit unit. Here are some guidelines.

Forgive the Opposing Influence

The whole principle of the gospel lies in loving and forgiving. Yet often, as we harbor feelings of anguish after an outside influence has intruded on family values, we find forgiveness is difficult. By placing our faith in God, by building our lives around His Word through continual prayer, fellowship, and service, we can experience the strength to forgive those who try to force their values on us. This *agape,* or selfless love, becomes real as we generate acceptance, forgiveness, and growth, and as we place our ultimate faith in God instead of humankind.

Your child can learn love and acceptance when outside influences interfere with family rules. The idea of "loving the sinner, but not the sin" is significant for your child as he learns to live in the world. We must teach our children that they might live differently than friends, and their faith will reflect in the choices they make—in friends, movies, television shows; where they spend their money and time; in the jokes they listen to; and the language they use. Yet we must also teach them that they can do it in a way that honors Christ and inspires others rather than condemning them.

Encourage Children to Stand on Their Own Beliefs

As your teen approaches young adulthood, communication in the home increases in importance. Teens at this age are usually very social and spend evenings with friends of both sexes. They also face much opposition, including friends and acquaintances who have different values and religious beliefs, and they must make decisions involving drugs and alcohol, sex, smoking, and more. The choices they make at this stage can affect them and others for a lifetime.

Let your older teen know he can talk with you *before* a problem arises. Being approachable means not lecturing when a teen discusses sensitive subjects such as drug and alcohol abuse or premarital sex. Let him air his views, then offer your opinion in love. Tell him how substance abuse can make him lose control of his senses—as well as his mind, coordination, and reasoning. Talk about the repercussions of teenage sex, from the life sentence of sexually transmitted diseases like AIDS to unwanted pregnancies.

Give your teen pamphlets from the American Cancer Society on the hazards of cigarette smoking, and be a smoke-free home. Model abstinence from alcohol and illegal drugs in your home. Young people respect parents who send the message, "Do as I do," instead of merely, "Do as I say." The best way to encourage a drug-free child is to be drug free yourself.

Some parents find it helpful to give teens ready answers to use when peer pressure gets so strong it's difficult to say no. Often that quick response can save a teen from making a life-threatening mistake under pressure. Here are several:

- This is against my Christian faith.

- I have promised God that I will not smoke (drink alcohol, have premarital sex).

- Sorry, I'm allergic to smoke (alcohol).

- My parents are paranoid. They smell my breath when I get home.

- I'm into health and fitness. That doesn't fit my routine.

- My parents are so strict they will ground me for even thinking about alcohol (smoking, drugs, sex).

This is not to let your teen put the responsibility somewhere else. When persuasive peers put the pressure on, teens need to know what to say—ahead of time. For some who are timid and easily led, practicing these statements gives them more strength than just saying no, only to be talked into something they really don't want to do.

Older teens are becoming equipped to stand on their own beliefs, but they still mess up from time to time. Become an advocate for forgiveness. If your teen wavers in his personal standards by testing his limits, use this time to help your child and to unite as a family. Many teens will continue to test your message to see if what you are saying is really true—simply because they are still children. Accepting and loving those who have committed wrong is what our Lord preached and lived. As Christian parents, we can carry this message of unconditional love and forgiveness to those in our homes.

Teach Your Child to Be a Peacemaker

Conflict is one form of opposition that we all face in our families, at school, or in the workplace. Sometimes strife erupts between two parents, resulting in separation or divorce. Your child and a best friend may take opposing sides of an issue during a heated debate, resulting in one going home. Even in loving families, arguments between siblings or between parent and child can cause tension and despair.

The good news: conflict is not new. Even in the earliest days of the church, people experienced the difficulty of facing conflict and finding a peaceful solution. Paul affirmed the unity of Christians (even though we differ in many ways) in Romans 12:5: "We, though many, are one body in Christ" (RSV).

Paul was well aware of diversity in the church. He saw Christians with different gifts: prophecy, service, teaching, exhortation, giving, acting with mercy (Rom. 12:6–7). He saw a church with different offices and functions: apostles, prophets, evangelists, pastors, and teachers (Eph. 4:11). To his distress, Paul also noticed the rise of divisive loyalties in the church: "I belong to Paul . . . to Apollos . . . to Cephas . . . to Christ" (1 Cor. 1:12, RSV). Yet Paul insisted that the church of Jesus Christ is one body. Like the human body, it needs different kinds of members—feet, hands, ears, eyes. But the church is defined by its unity, not its diversity.

As Christians, we can choose to make peace with those who oppose us in life or we can choose to keep peace—and there is a world of difference between the two.

A *peacekeeper avoids the issue at hand,* resorting to any technique available to ease the conflict. This avoidance of the problem merely satisfies the opponents temporarily, for tension likely will return. A peacekeeper may compromise his values, ideas, or morals just to make others happy. Often a peacekeeper runs from the very situation that creates conflict in his life, feeling that this will resolve the problem. In contrast, a *peacemaker seeks to solve conflict.* She chooses to hear all sides of the problem and searches intently for the truth. This search involves listening, weighing the arguments, and taking a stand—often one that is *not* popular. Yet being a peacemaker is a risk. Someone is sure to become angry when his view is challenged. Being a peacemaker, however, is part of our challenge as Christ's disciples. Jesus Christ was a peacemaker. He wasn't concerned with winning a popularity contest. Rather, as He sought to share God's love and principles of fairness and equality, He made many enemies of people who felt intimidated by truth.

As our children mature in their spiritual walk with Jesus Christ, we must teach them that peacemaking is the way of our Lord. Going that extra mile to be a peacemaker in the family or school can be a risk. Often, when children seek to reveal the truth in conflicts, they risk being disliked by some.

When anyone takes a stand, especially an unpopular stand, she will often be ostracized by friends or loved ones. Teaching our children to be advocates for issues and circumstances they know to be true can also be a challenge.

Yet as they deepen their spiritual awareness, their lives will begin to reflect true caring and concern for those around them as they take on the role of peacemaker. As peacemakers, they will experience cooperation as they learn to work together and trust each other. As peacemakers, they will communicate with others in a Christlike manner as they listen with compassion and sensitivity to each other. As Christians making peace, they will become tolerant as they respect each other's views and differences and work together for the best solution.

WHEN OPPOSITION SEEMS ENDLESS . . .
FINISH THE RACE!

The secret of life parents must convey to their children is this: It's not where you begin that's important, but where you finish. Sometimes that means you keep on keeping on when it would be much easier to throw up your hands in despair and walk away. That means that you hang in there and see it through when a person of lesser determination or lesser courage would seek an escape. That applies to all areas of life, whether dealing with an obstinate friend, coping with a contrary teacher, or fighting a chronic illness. An aging Winston Churchill put it this way in a speech to young men: "You men, never give up! Never give up! Never! Never! Never!" Paul never gave up when he was up against the odds. In spite of shipwrecks, numerous beatings, and imprisonments, he remained faithful to his calling to be an evangelist, a missionary, a preacher of the good news of Jesus Christ. He could look back over his life with satisfaction and say, "I have fought the good fight, I have finished the race, I have kept the faith. Henceforth there is laid up for me a crown of righteousness" (2 Tim. 4:7–8, RSV). What lessons can you teach your children when they're up against the odds and it seems endless?

It makes no difference how much talent or natural ability we may have—or lack. To excel requires extraordinary effort. Remember the great athlete named "Babe" Didrikson Zaharias? In the 1932 Olympics, she placed first in the women's eighty-meter hurdles, first in the javelin throw, and second in the high jump. She was also superb in baseball and basketball. Then she turned to golf, where she also became a world champion. Natural ability? Most certainly. Yet there was much more! When "the Babe" took up golf, she sought out an exceptionally fine instructor. She studied the game, analyzed her golf swing, dissected it, and tested each component part until she understood it thoroughly. When she went on a practice tee, she would practice as much as twelve hours a day, hitting as many as a thousand balls in an afternoon. She would swing—and keep swinging—until her hands were so sore she could scarcely grip a club. She would stop long enough to tape her hands before picking up her club again. That's the method she used to perfect her powerful swing.

Few things of real value in life are acquired without effort or determination, especially when it seems the opposition will never cease. It took Kenneth Taylor six years to convert portions of the New Testament into a format nearly everyone could read easily. The first publisher he sent it to flatly rejected it. So did a second and a third. Finally, he used his savings and published it himself, but only 800 copies were sold the first year. Still Taylor didn't quit. He continued the tedious business of translating and paraphrasing the entire Bible while seeking a publisher. Today, more than 25 million copies of Taylor's work have been sold. You may have a copy in your home. It's *The Living Bible*.

Paul persevered when the odds were against him. Babe Zaharias gave everything that she had. Kenneth Taylor's determination to provide *The Living Bible* for Christians was a study in excellence. These people could look back with satisfaction, not only because they had "fought the fight," but because it was a "good fight." *That is the meaning of character.* You can teach your child to develop this character as he learns to say, "I had some tough breaks, and I had some heartbreaks along the way, but I gave it my best!" Such dedication will always earn reward.

The saddest of all conditions is to have no real purpose for which to live. Paul had a purpose—a purpose that helped him persevere when every earthly helper had forsaken him. He had a purpose that drove him to excellence in all things—even when it didn't seem to matter. His purpose was to serve Christ! That same purpose is what we must teach our children.

No matter what happens in your child's life—he falls off his bicycle, she loses the race, he fails a test, she breaks up with her boyfriend—the service of Christ is for all eternity. Paul writes about the prize: "Henceforth there is laid up for me the crown of righteousness, which the Lord, the righteous judge, will award to me on that Day, and not only to me but also to all who have loved his appearing" (2 Tim. 4:8, RSV).

In the Christian life, finishing is everything. This life is but a prelude; the symphony is yet to begin! That is the message of the gospel. This world is but a preparatory school for the real world yet to come.

GAINING STRENGTH TO FINISH THE RACE

Parents can encourage children to stand strong amidst the world's values. Let's review some ways to do so.

Keep Communication Open in Your Home

Let your child know that she can talk to you if she has concerns about opposing values or obstacles she might face in the world. Being approachable means not lecturing when your child discusses the subject; but letting her speak, then offering your opinion in love.

Be an Active Family Unit

Starting when your child is just a toddler, let your home be the "Kool-Aid" home. Plan activities for your child and his friends at your home, and provide a place for the children to sit, talk, play, and just "be."

Get to Know Your Child's Friends

As your child matures, it becomes even more vital to get to know her friends. Invite them over for snacks, or treat them to dinner at a local hangout. Become interested in their music, activities, and sports events. Watch for symptoms that may surface in a companion, indicating that things may not be suitable for your child. If you feel a peer is a negative influence, discuss your feelings and fears openly with your child.

Continue Table Talks

If you are engaging in Table Talks—as discussed in previous chapters—use the following ideas to talk about opposing influences and your family's values:

Talk about your family's personal standards and values. Write some of these down on a piece of paper and hang this on the refrigerator. Ask your children to watch for situations in their lives that challenge or conflict with your standards, and talk about these at dinner time.

Share with your child times when you felt challenged by the beliefs of others and how you handled it. These recollections could be when you were a teen or even a recent time. Your child needs to know that standing strong for what she believes is an honorable attribute and adds to character and integrity.

Give your child a sheet of paper and ask him to write down behaviors in his life that are right and wrong. A younger child may tell you what is right or wrong instead of writing it. For example:

Right	**Wrong**
obeying my parents	talking back
respecting my teacher	making fun of friends
doing my own homework	cheating on tests
loving my sister and brother	hurting people

Talk with your child about this list and ask, "How do you know what is right and what is wrong?" Let him know that when God is in our life, He gives us direction for making the right choices.

ALWAYS STAY IN THE CHURCH

A youth agency seemed to have the perfect formula for dealing with the evil influences of society with a colorful wall poster that read, *Win Against Crime: God and Family.* Make church attendance and membership important in your home. Teach your child that this commitment to Christ's church is vital to his spiritual development and moral strength. Not only will your child grow from biblical teaching, but he also will see you as a Christlike role model and have a strong support system to turn to when the forces against him seem too strong.

SPIRITUAL FOOD FOR THOUGHT

1. What importance does television have in your family's life? Do you watch some shows that have non-Christian values?

2. Make a list of five criteria for watching television shows, movies, or videos that are in keeping with Christ's teachings. Share this list with your children.

3. Think of opposing influences in your family's life. Talk about these with your children. What stand do you and your children need to take to stand strong as Christians?

4. Is there a cost to being a Christian today? How can we take up our cross and stand strong when faced with worldly temptations? What opposition might we face when we do this?

5. Write down three temptations in your life that make it difficult to focus on your relationship with Jesus Christ. Keep this list with you this week and pray to God for strength in overcoming the odds in your life.

Nine

Teaching Your Child about Death

It seemed to happen within weeks: Brittnye's cat was hit by a car, and Rob's newborn gerbils died. The favorite dog that roamed the neighborhood was found dead early one morning when we went for a walk. Then a close friend died without any warning. In each of these painful instances, the question we asked was: "What will we tell the children?"

No matter how hard you might want to protect your child from experiencing the trauma of death, it's a reality everyone will face. Though we can't predict when death will come to a loved one, we can prepare ourselves emotionally and spiritually to handle this life event with our children.

In many families, the subject of death is taboo. One friend told us how she would never let her children attend a funeral for fear it would make them sad. Yet when their grandfather died suddenly while visiting them, the children were overwhelmed with anxiety and fear as they experienced something so foreign to them.

Death is a part of life, and you need to talk openly about it with your child just as you would with any other subject. No matter what their age, children need to understand that death is a natural part of our life cycle, not something terrible or a punishment that happens when people are bad or disobedient to God. Simply put, death occurs when our physical bodies wear out or stop functioning. Sometimes death comes tragically to children or adults from sickness or accidents. Other times it claims innocent victims—babies, children, and parents—from catastrophes such as a hurricane or earthquake; or it claims them through poverty, hunger, violence, and war. Most of the time, though, death happens when people have lived a long life and are very old.

As you explain death to your child, distinguish between the *physical and the spiritual body*. When a Christian dies, it is the physical body, their shell, that is sealed in a casket and buried in the ground. Their spiritual body, their soul, goes on to live eternally with our heavenly Father. This is a difficult concept even for adults to comprehend, but with openness supported by your faith in Jesus Christ, you will be able to help your child begin to understand death.

THE MYSTERY OF DEATH

If adults struggle to comprehend the mystery of death, think how difficult it is to answer children's questions. One of the best comparisons is to the birth process. Delia Halverson, author of *How Do Our Children Grow?*, suggests asking children if they remember what it felt like before they were born. Explain that a baby is very happy in the mother's womb. Coming into the world must be a very scary experience because the baby doesn't know what to expect. Death is much like that for us. We don't know exactly what to expect. Yet we can always rely on the plan that our loving God has made for us. Our experience of life has shown us that the rest of God's plan is all wise and all loving; we know that we can depend on Him.[1]

Death certainly catches us off guard. It is interesting how surprised we are when death takes a friend or loved one. Most of us live as if we are going to be healthy and alive forever. Yet the reality of life is that *all of us are going to die.* As Christians we believe that death moves us from life on earth to another life—an eternal one. Facing death as part of life, and sharing the burden of sorrow, along with the hope of eternal life, is vital teaching for our children. It needs to be shared in the context of the Christian faith with the promises that it holds.

LIVING IN A STERILE SOCIETY

It is sad that death in our society has become so sterile, so far removed from the course of everyday events. Not so long ago, most people died at home, and families, including the youngest child, were involved in the process all along. Grandparents tell of the time when family members would die, and the body would be placed in the parlor of the home. Friends and neighbors would come from afar to pay their respects to the dead person and his grieving family, bringing gifts of baked goods and helping with the household chores.

Yet with medical advances in recent years, the death process has become increasingly institutionalized. Many people die in a sterile hospital bed surrounded by tubes, machines, and strangers instead of at home with loved ones. This modern ritual tends to hide the reality of death from our children. In our ministry, we have met many people who are well into their adult years and *have never attended a funeral nor seen a dead person.*

Our culture seems determined to hide the fact that *death is part of life.* We hide the sick and the infirm away in hospitals and nursing homes. When death comes, it usually occurs behind closed doors. Sometimes even the rituals of funerals shelter us from the reality of death, and we sweep the whole issue under the rug.

THE FEELINGS OF DEATH

It is never easy to accept death. When a loved one dies, adults and children alike may feel angry, confused, or emotionally numb.

We may not know how to express our feelings of loss, or how to say good-bye to the person who has died. Yet teaching children that death is part of life is where the parents' values and beliefs come into play.

Often the greatest spiritual growth emerges from times of pain and loss. Many people have experienced the truth of British minister, psychologist, and author, Leslie Weatherhead's observation: "Like all people, I love and prefer the sunny uplands of experience, when health, happiness and success abound, but I have learned more about God, life and myself in the darkness of fear and failure than I have ever learned in the sunshine. . . . The darkness, thank God, passes. But what one learns in the darkness, one possesses forever."[2]

Understanding Death

While death is an unavoidable reality, parents can give their children the strength of faith so it is not a crippling experience. How can you enable your child to better understand the part of life we call death?

Communicate with your child about death. While there are no easy answers to death, a parent can create an atmosphere of love and acceptance as the family talks openly about death. Depending on your child's understanding, explain to her that death is the name we give to a part of life that is unknown and confusing. You may talk about the leaves on trees that die in wintertime, or mention how the flowers in the vase have all died. As you answer children's questions regarding the death of an acquaintance or loved one, don't tell them that someone is "sleeping" or has "moved to be with God." This is misleading to children. Although death can make us sad or even angry, the more we accept it as a part of life and explain it to our children, the better we will feel.

Sometimes death doesn't seem fair, as when a close friend or grandparent dies. During those times we feel as if God must be against us to make us so very sad. Yet talking about these feelings of sadness or anger or confusion is important to finally accepting the reality of the loss.

Children react differently to death. At ages two to six, they think death is reversible. A child might say, "Grandma went away, but she'll come back in time for my birthday." Or he might just think that the dead person is merely sleeping or tired. Death becomes frightening for children ages six to nine. They don't understand this mystery, and may react by asking if they can touch the person's eyes to see what they feel like. Or they may cry and appear fearful at the funeral because it is so foreign to them. Death is disruptive to children ages nine to twelve. Children of this age have a greater awareness of what is happening when someone dies and know that the person will never come back. Death is painful for teenagers. When a friend, grandparent, or even a parent dies, a teenager might express his grief in anger or even disillusionment with life as a loved one leaves.[3]

Face the reality of death in your family. Realize that death will come into your life. Acknowledge the fact that you will one day be leaving this life for the next. Therefore, live the very best you can now, in order that you will have no regrets when the end comes. Let your children know that death is a reality for all people, and encourage them to live so that each day counts. This is such a challenge for most people—to treat each day on earth as if it was our last. Yet this challenge can help alleviate any guilt feelings when a loved one dies as we live each day sharing Jesus' love and compassion.

Don't hesitate to take your child to funerals. One of the most common questions people ask us is, "Should we take our child to a funeral?" They fear their child seeing adults crying or being sad. Yet funerals can help us to work through our feelings.

A funeral also is a ritual that can bring meaning to the experience of death. Rituals link us to the past and the future. We have rituals for baptisms, graduations, and marriages, and we need a ritual for death, the last passage of life. A funeral commemorates the deceased; but just as importantly, it helps the survivors to heal emotionally. When someone we love dies, we experience the pain of grief. Yet even though it hurts, grief is not something to avoid. This is important for our children to learn. Grief, in fact, is the very part of the healing process that allows us to separate ourselves from the deceased person and to move on with our lives.

Funerals give people a ritual to express their feelings of sadness and loss. They also stimulate people to begin talking about the deceased, one of the first steps toward accepting death. In fact, people who don't attend the funeral of a loved one because they want to deny the death may suffer from unresolved grief months later. To resolve their grief, people need to accept the reality of death, not only on an intellectual level but also on an emotional one. That is why many funerals in our culture are preceded by an open-casket visitation period. Research has found that the viewing of the deceased helps you to accept the death of that person.

Talk about the victory of death for a Christian. Realizing that death is a vital part of living allows us to face life victoriously as we love others for the moment, instead of waiting to share personal feelings or concern. As you explain the Christian perspective of death to your child, remember that each child differs in his or her response to the subject of death depending on personal experiences, knowledge, and maturity. Emphasize the teachings of Jesus Christ and God's Word. Share the reality that God gives us strength and courage in times of darkness and sustains us even when we are at the lowest point.

Explain eternal life in terms your child can understand. Talk openly about how life seems unfair, especially when a young friend dies. Yet Christians have the assurance of life eternal. While our physical body is no longer here, our spirit lives with Jesus Christ.

When Ashley's childhood friend died several years ago, we emphasized the teachings of Jesus Christ and God's Word as she tried to understand why Peter was no longer able to play with her.

"Peter has been promised eternal life because he was a Christian," we told her. "This promise is for all believers and is the hope of our Christian faith." At age eleven, Ashley didn't understand the awesomeness of this truth, but she did understand that Peter was with the Lord and that he was not alone nor in pain. Her upbringing in the church and her wealth of instruction in the faith gave her strength and a greater understanding than if she had no faith.

Eternal life is promised for all believers. If you are confident in what you believe, you will radiate truth and assurance to your children as you discuss death in your family.

Give your child straightforward answers when someone dies. Closed doors, whispering, and sending the child off to a neighbor's house when someone dies in your family only adds to the fear of the unknown. That is why it's best to talk openly before a loved one dies. Instigate conversation about a pet or plant that has died. This will enable your child to open up with concerns, worries, and feelings. Sharing memories of loved ones who have died also can open up conversations about death. This enables your child to reaffirm that people will live on in our minds.

One of the things that helped Ashley work through her friend's death was talking about her cat who had died just months before. "I still think of Buffy every night," she told us one evening as we tucked her into bed. "I still pretend I'm holding her and even laugh as I remember the silly things she did with me."

"And you will have those wonderful thoughts about Peter, too," we assured her. "You might cry when you think about him and miss him, but you will still giggle when you think of the time you and Peter ate the cookie dough out of my bowl and blamed it on Brittnye, or when you played hide-and-seek and kickball after dusk during the summer. You will never forget Peter just like you haven't forgotten Buffy."

Relating death to the loss of a pet enabled her to open up. Ashley was able to see that even though loved ones leave us, they will still live on in our hearts and minds.

Help your child express her feelings. Expressing feelings is an important part of the healing process. Many feelings accompany the stages of grief, including denial, anger, sadness, guilt, fear, blame, and finally acceptance.

If your child has these feelings of guilt, anger, or fear, let him know it's OK to cry. Allow him to see you cry. Give him the words they need to express emotions. If a child seems to ignore the conversation at first, drop it and try again later. Let him talk about the person who has died and affirm the feelings he shares.[4]

Talk to your child about the sadness he feels after a pet dies. While the sadness might feel as if it will never go away, it will diminish in time. Compare this sadness to the pain of a cut finger. At first the finger hurts very badly. Yet each day, as the cut heals, the pain lessens.

After telling our children that Peter had died, we encouraged them to talk about Peter and his illness, and we emphasized how God was in control of his life.

After Peter's death, Ashley came to us with a beautiful letter she had written a few days before he died. In the letter she told Peter what a wonderful best friend he was and how she thanked him for being patient with her when she was so bossy. She drew a picture of Peter and herself throwing a ball. She had taped a stick of gum as a get-well offering.

"Now he'll never get to read my letter, Mommy," she cried.

Knowing that we couldn't turn back time, we encouraged Ashley to put the letter in an envelope and give it to his parents as a remembrance of their son, her dearest friend. Even though Peter never read the letter, it was on display in his home as friends and relatives came to pay their respect. His family appreciated that someone so young cared deeply for their son.

Realize that each child is different in his interpretation and response. Each child understands the subject of death differently, depending on his experiences, knowledge, and maturity. Some may react to death with anger, hostility, or even aggression. Some may withdraw or become sullen and silent. Still others may react with nonstop crying. At a funeral, children may say inappropriate things about the dead person, or they might want to feel the body to see what being dead feels like. Rather than becoming angry at their questions or comments, help them to understand what is happening. Imagine how foreign this experience is to a child.

By coping with problems our children become strong and resilient. While we cannot bring the dead person back, we can add comfort. After we told our children about Peter's death, each child reacted differently. Our oldest son accepted the news without any open display of emotion, yet spent the afternoon riding his bike for miles. "I felt so angry at Peter and his doctors, and even God," he told us later. "I couldn't believe that all those grown-ups had let us down; they let Peter down."

Our daughters cried openly and wanted to help Peter's sisters. They spent the afternoon making cookies to take to them. Even though their responses were different, it was important that they talked about their feelings and worked through these emotions in appropriate ways.

Teach your child about the kingdom of heaven. Jesus taught that the kingdom of heaven is like a treasure hidden in a field, which a man found and then in his joy went and sold all he had and bought that field. The kingdom of heaven, Jesus added, is like a merchant in search of fine pearls, who, on finding one pearl of great value, went and sold all that he had and bought it. The Bible tells us that heaven has gates of pearls, streets of gold, and foundations adorned with jewels (see Rev. 21:18–21). As Christians, we believe that heaven is the ultimate in living, with beauty far beyond our imagination. Heaven is a real place where we will live in communion with God and Jesus Christ.

Let your child know that heaven is a wonderful place, and that it far surpasses any earthly treasures. Explain to your child that in heaven there is no death, no sadness, no tears, no hurt nor pain. In heaven, people who love one another and who love Jesus will always be together. God, our heavenly Father, will be there, along with all of the angels. Joy and laughter will take the place of sadness and tears.

When a person dies, he or she cannot live with us here on earth, and that makes us sad. Yet because of Jesus, that person can have eternal life in heaven. Someday we will join that person and live with him and all our family and friends.[5]

After experiencing the death of her best friend, Ashley wrote the following words to describe what heaven must be like:

Heaven Is a Wonderful Place!

I have always wondered what heaven might be like. I have heard different stories about heaven. People have told me that it has no age, time, race, boys or girls. I have also heard that it is full of joy and love; there is no unhappiness and no one disrespects anyone or anything—even the slightest bit!

There supposedly aren't any physical forms of bodies, just wonderful spirits and equality. I believe that if you love the Lord with your whole heart, even for as little as a minute, you will go to heaven. But if you never love God, you will just die and probably never go anywhere or have an eternal life.

Some people say that heaven might be "too much of a change," and these people don't want to go to heaven to be totally happy.

I agree. Heaven would be a big change, but once you enter this lovely place, it will be so wonderful that you won't ever want to go back out.

Remember, death is not an ending. If you believe in Christ, it is just the beginning.

Ashley Elizabeth Bruce, age 11

EASTER PEOPLE, COME TOGETHER!

Easter tells us that *God is involved in our world.* At Eastertime, we celebrate a victorious life in Christ Jesus; and we learn that more than anything else, people matter. You see, Christianity is not simply a set of values, a moral code, or grand philosophy of life. The Christian faith is an Easter faith. It is the conviction that people matter so much to God that He gave up His own Son in our behalf. He allowed His Son to be crucified on the cross for our sins, and on the third day, God raised His Son from the grave as a sign and symbol that our lives are of eternal significance to Him. God is involved in our lives. Christ is victorious. And . . . we really do matter to God.

That is why the empty tomb is central to our faith. Throughout the centuries men have tried to honor their heroes by erecting lavish monuments—the massive pyramids, built as resting places for the Egyptian pharaohs, India's glistening Taj Mahal; Lenin's Tomb in Moscow's Red Square.

In its stark simplicity, Jesus' grave can't compare with these costly crypts. But the tomb of Jesus excels in the most important respect: It stands empty. He is not there. Jesus Christ is alive, and death has been conquered. We can lift our eyes from our problems to the possibilities. Christ is alive, and because He lives, we also can live. Our faith in Jesus Christ, who promised that He has prepared a place for us, calls us to reevaluate and courageously participate in the drama of life. Death is a part of that drama.

Let us then live and love boldly for God and plan ahead for the greatest adventure of all: the transition into life eternal, which God has prepared for all who love Him and who are called according to His purpose.

SPIRITUAL FOOD FOR THOUGHT

1. Have you talked openly about death with your children? What fears or concerns are holding you back from teaching them about this natural part of life?

2. If your children have never attended the funeral of a loved one, make it a point to take them to a funeral while they are still young. This may be the funeral of a family member,

friend, or church member. Let them see this as a celebration of life, and talk about the feelings they might share.

3. Has your child lost a pet? Make plans to celebrate the animal's life with a funeral service—even if it was several years ago when it died. At the service, let your child share memories of the pet and how special it was.

4. Read Ecclesiastes 3:1–14 with your child. Talk about the seasons of life. Has a new baby been born in your family or to a friend? Talk about the excitement and joy of waiting for the new birth. Compare this to the sadness and loneliness we feel when a friend or loved one dies as we miss their presence. Let your child know that all feelings are normal and a part of our life.

5. Look through a family photo album with your child. Talk about the wonderful memories you have of people who have died. Let your child know that just because someone is not here with us, we still can remember and love them.

Ten

Put Feet to Faith

When our friend Candy came over one day and sat at the table in our kitchen, we thought she had lost her best friend.

"Pete's thirtieth birthday was yesterday," she said with a sigh as she stirred her coffee. "I had thought about having a big surprise party with all of his close friends. I even called a caterer to price the meal and bought the cutest invitations. But the twins are teething, and Kimmie demands so much of my time. I just never went through with the plans."

We both empathized with her. We also have been full of wonderful intentions to care for others, such as the day Deb phoned to volunteer at the school carnival but forgot to write it on her calendar. Or the day Bob promised to take the kids to the high school basketball game but scheduled a church committee meeting instead. Both times we got so wrapped up in life's little interruptions that loving actions were forgotten.

While good intentions are admirable, without action, they have no meaning. Our salvation is totally God's work in Christ, but authentic faith must find its expression in love. Works become the result and consequence of faith.[1]

It has been said that we make a living by what we get out of life, but we make a life by what we give. John challenges us to begin a lifestyle of good intentions *and* deeds: "Little children, let us stop just saying we love people; let us really love them, and show it by our actions" (1 John 3:18, TLB).

As parents, we both know how difficult it is to be kind and thoughtful when days are filled with kids, carpools, commitments, and chaos, but evangelism for our Lord can take place only when we care for others with the self-less *agape* love that Jesus taught. We must put feet to faith. Teaching your child that kind of love will strengthen her faith in a benevolent God and help her become a powerful spiritual witness to those around her.

BE GOOD AND DO GOOD

Spirituality, broadly defined, is the impulse to be good and to do good. It gives us a sense of optimism that can carry us through difficult times. Spirituality imparts a feeling of oneness with others and a reverence for and appreciation of life.[2]

Being a Christian witness starts at home as children learn to reach out beyond themselves and minister to others—siblings, parents, friends, neighbors—in a way that will touch them in their lives. As our children begin to emerge spiritually, they may seek to help others more as a result of a growing, authentic faith. They may take such actions as helping a new child at school, being kinder to a sibling, offering to help around the home without being asked, or taking cookies to a neighbor who is ill.

Teaching our children to pray, to read the Bible, and to have a regular devotional life are the basics for a Christian walk. Yet the essence of a devotional life is cultivating an awareness of the presence of God and living in a posture of listening to God. We listen by many means—reading the Bible, praying, talking with other believers, attending sermons, journaling, worshiping. It is easy, though, to fall into the mistaken idea that listening alone is enough, that we are most spiritual when we sit silently before God, waiting for inspiration and direction. Still, there comes a time when we also must act. We must respond to God's nudgings if we are to be faithful.[3]

Here are some ways you can teach your child to respond to God's nudgings while putting feet to faith.

Set Goals for Your Family

The home is the first place young Christians can learn to touch the lives of others with Christ's love and personal caring. Gather your family together and establish ways members can help each other at home. What behaviors do members need to work on for family harmony? What needs do certain members have this week that others could assist with? Write these ideas down on paper and put them on the refrigerator. After a few days, meet again and evaluate your family's progress. Remember: "A house divided against itself will not stand" (Matt. 12:25, RSV). This reminds us of the importance of starting at home with the family to live your faith.

Talk about the Importance of Giving

God loves a cheerful giver (2 Cor. 9:7). As you teach your child to give to others, you will help her reflect the true meaning of faith.

At your family meeting, read Bible verses that present good models of giving. Read about the boy who shared his lunch (John 6:1–13) and the poor widow's offering (Luke 21:2–3) from a Bible storybook. Then ask your child to name some specific ways he can show love by giving to others. Write these suggestions down.

Create a "Giving Tree" with your child's ideas. Ask him to write each idea on colored paper and cut them in leaf shapes. Help him to draw the shape of a tree on cardboard or stiff paper, then attach the leaves to the tree.[4]

Display the tree in a family room or near the dining table. Add a new leaf to the tree each day with an additional idea. Let your child pick a leaf before breakfast each day and perform the act of giving described.

Try Random Acts of Kindness

You can teach your child to put feet to faith and be a good Samaritan as you challenge him to do random acts of kindness each day. Explain to your child that acts of kindness are as common as a cold and can be caught just as easily. Use the following list as challenges for your child to brighten someone's day:

- taking your plate to the kitchen after dinner

- making his sister's bed

- not talking back to parents

- doing a chore without being reminded

- helping to wash vegetables for dinner

- walking a neighbor's dog after school

- washing dishes for the family

- taking out the trash without being asked

- reading to a younger brother

- picking up toys without being asked

- washing the car

- vacuuming the den

- writing letters to grandparents

- taking food to a neighbor who is ill

- reading a Bible story to the family at dinnertime

- making cards for church members who are hospitalized

- serving Mom and Dad breakfast in bed
- letting someone get ahead in the lunch line at school
- complimenting a friend
- refusing to get angry with a brother or sister
- apologizing to a friend who is angry with you
- doing a chore for a sibling without her knowing about it
- inviting a new friend to come home after school
- being extra kind to a teacher
- standing up for your faith with friends at school
- picking up the litter on the street
- calling a friend who is lonely
- writing a Bible verse on paper and memorizing it
- sharing this Bible verse at dinnertime
- recycling the family's trash each day
- forgiving a friend who has wronged you
- playing with a child who seems lonely
- thinking positive thoughts
- telling a friend about Jesus
- praying for a friend
- writing a thank-you note to a friend
- encouraging someone who is worried
- smiling at a new child at school
- offering to help a teacher without being asked

Giving to the Needy

The elementary school years are the perfect time to encourage acts of charity by your child. Children at this age know what is right, even though parents would argue they don't always do what is right! Realize the compassionate nature of this age, and teach your child that giving to the needy can be incorporated into daily life.

Here are several ways you and your child can become involved in the spirit of giving.

Talk about giving to the needy with your child. Ask your child to go through her closet, toy boxes, and shelves and give away any unwanted toys, puzzles, cassette tapes, stuffed animals, or even good clothing. Many organizations in town will come to your home to pick these up. Try to arrange this pickup time for after-school hours when your child is at home, so she can appreciate the inner warmth of generosity.

Call a volunteer organization in your community. Ask if you and your child could help distribute food, clothing, or toys before Christmas or during the holidays when the child is out of school. Most large cities have at least one volunteer organization, such as the United Way, listed in the phone book that can direct you to groups that need extra hands during this season. Your church may also have special programs for the needy, such as a toy or food drive, and could use extra help. This can be an enriching experience for children as they see others in need and feel a genuine part of helping.

Ask your pastor for the name of a shut-in. Help your child make a glittery Christmas card and plate of decorated cookies. Take these to a shut-in and spend a few minutes enjoying fellowship and Christmas carols. Don't let your child's benevolence stop with a holiday; take her back again, perhaps on a monthly basis, to visit this person.

Through your church or a local social agency, ask for the name of a family in need and provide a special dinner for them. With your child's assistance, you can take a meal along with canned goods to the family. If it is during Christmas time and funds are available, purchase a few small gifts for the family members and let your child wrap them. He may want to decorate Christmas cookies for this family. Not only will the needy family experience joy, but you and your child will bond as you work on a project for others.

Help Your Child to Be on Mission

Today millions of senior adults are confined at home, in nursing homes, or in other institutions. They are there for many reasons including illness, physical or mental handicaps, lack of transportation, or other personal problems.

These elderly people have the same emotional and spiritual needs as all of us. You can help your children learn about giving to others as you involve them in service. The list is endless of things we can do to take care of the homebound in our community, and the rewards to you and your child will be eternal.

Take one Saturday a month to visit a nearby nursing or retirement home with your family. You might provide copies of a devotional guide (large print preferred) for the residents.

While you are visiting, help your child assist someone with a task that person can no longer do. This can include writing letters to family members, decorating the room, or folding clothes neatly. This can boost the compassion of even the youngest child as he helps someone else.

Help your child "adopt" one person in a nursing home. Visit this person more frequently, taking baked treats and small gifts. Make sure your child helps to create the gift or treat and gives this to the person, so he can take ownership in the project.

Provide the person with taped sermons from your church. Videotapes would also be greatly appreciated if the homebound person has access to a VCR.

Make sure shut-ins have tapes of hymns and songs. This inspiration will help them feel joy and fellowship even when you and your child aren't present with them.

Help your child write a note, draw a colorful picture, or call the "adopted" friend each week. A few lines on a piece of paper or a few minutes on the phone will help this person feel loved and included. Encourage other family members to do the same.

Recognize the homebound person's birthday or anniversary with a small party. Bring a cake or other foods that the homebound person can eat. Let your child share the spirit of Christian giving with a card or gift.

Touching is vital for human beings. Yet often the elderly are ignored when it comes to gentle hugs or holding hands. When you visit, show your child how to use the healing power of touch as she relates to her "adopted" friend.

VOLUNTEER TO SERVE

The opportunities for your older child or teen to reach beyond himself and volunteer to help others are tremendous. Volunteers of all ages are the vitality and strength of hospitals, churches, community organizations, schools, and charities. Being a volunteer can help your child develop a sense of higher purpose in life.

Develop Empathy

The youth group at our church went to the coast of Louisiana as short-term volunteers. They helped the victims of Hurricane Andrew by replacing walls, painting houses, patching roofs, and more. One young teen summed up her experiences by saying: "I really thought everyone lived like me in an air-conditioned, clean home in the suburbs—until this work project. While I was painting the outside of a small wooden house in ninety-eight degree humid weather, I started praying for these victims and thanking God for my home and family. I can't wait to go back next summer and help these people, and I will never take my home for granted again."

Our son Rob spent the summer after his junior year as a "volunteen" at a children's clinic. His experiences in all the departments virtually changed his life at age sixteen. "While volunteering in physical therapy, I observed and played with the physically and mentally challenged children during their painful and difficult therapy," said Rob, now a senior in college. "It was so sad to see the condition of these children, but it touched my heart to see them make great progress while working so hard each day."

As volunteens, Rob and other youths participating in the program saw all types of illnesses and physical impairments. Yet they also saw health care professionals striving to improve the quality of life for their young patients. They experienced the difference teens can make in people's lives as they distracted them during painful therapy with games, laughter, and compassion.

Develop Commitment and Purpose

Twelve-year-old John told us how he and his twin brother did absolutely nothing for many days during the summer except sleep, eat, and swim. "Sure, we were bright and energetic the rest of the year," he said, "but we turned into total vegetables for the summer months—until our mom called a volunteer agency in our town.

"The woman at the agency placed both of us with the American Cancer Society as volunteers. We complained because we had to get up early every morning and go to the headquarters to assist with the campaign—stapling fliers, stuffing envelopes, running errands, answering phones, and more. But, quite honestly, we really felt important and were even given awards at the annual volunteer banquet. I think we are probably more compassionate people now."

Boost Confidence

When thirteen-year-old Miranda applied to be a candy striper at the city hospital, she rarely looked at the interviewer while speaking. "This was the shiest teenager I had ever seen, and I almost hesitated in letting her volunteer," the director said. "I was concerned that she could not handle meeting the patients."

Yet after spending many long days at the hospital helping young children with their meals and comforting elderly patients, Miranda has become a different person. "She comes in each morning just beaming," the director commented. "She speaks to everyone and doesn't hesitate to talk with any of the patients. She's been transformed."

Miranda claims the transformation came while volunteering one day. "I was always so afraid of what people thought about me," she said. "Was my hair messed up? Would I say the wrong thing? Then one day I was combing the hair of a little girl who just had surgery, and she told me I was the kindest lady she ever met. I felt so special! Since that time I decided I was OK just being me. I now love to go each day and see who I can be kind to."

Reaching out and caring for others helps children and teens to become focused on something other than self. Volunteering can boost confidence and self-esteem as they give back to society.

ENCOURAGE YOUR CHILD TO VOLUNTEER

Volunteer opportunities exist almost anywhere people need services and funds are limited. Many large cities have a volunteer agency (Volunteers in Action, Voluntary Action Center, Volunteer Bureau, United Way) that places willing people in different positions and services after an initial screening of talents and time. Large institutions and hospitals often handle their own volunteer placement, and usually have special clubs or groups just for teen volunteers. You may also call the guidance counselor at your teen's high school and ask for information on summer volunteering.

Keep in mind your child's schedule and talents as she commits to being a volunteer. If she is active, she probably will not enjoy answering phones all day. If she likes the out-of-doors, she should volunteer with the local YMCA or a day camp instead of an enclosed office. She may want to start with two days a week or just mornings until she decides if she enjoys this type of work.

Where to Find Volunteer Opportunities

You can find volunteer opportunities at the following places in your city:

- churches
- doctors' offices
- hospitals
- nursing homes
- community organizations
- hot-line and crisis centers
- charitable organizations (Red Cross, United Way)
- halfway houses
- YMCA, YWCA
- children's homes
- schools and day-care centers
- zoos

STIMULATE GLOBAL AWARENESS

As you teach your child to put feet to faith, you can stimulate global awareness at home. Ideas such as taping maps on the wall in a "mission corner" in the kitchen or child's bedroom, a globe with flags pinned on locations where your church supports missionaries, or asking missionaries to correspond with your child can all encourage a global awareness in your home.

Take your children to mission rallies at your church. Show them films about living conditions of the mission field. Take them on field trips to local places where mission support is being given (such as a local homeless shelter or homebuilding with Habitat for Humanity).

Other ideas:

- "Adopt" an overseas child through a mission program that provides aid to this child's family.

- Have an empty jar on the kitchen table to collect all undesignated change. Give these funds to your church to help a missionary in a Third-World country or for an inner-city ministry in your area.

- Give your child a folder with appropriate slots to save a dime a day. Collect the money after a period of time and send to church-sponsored missionaries.

- Go through your child's toys and clothing with him and ask him to give quality items to needy children overseas.

Temporary Trustees

Another way we can teach our children to put feet to faith is to be responsible stewards of God's earth. Don't we all enjoy the bounty of goods that God has provided? We must teach our children that everything—all that we have and are—belongs to God. You see, God has made us the temporary trustees of His world. To see God in nature, our relationship with nature must be renewed. This means turning off video games, televisions, and computers, and spending time outdoors as you encourage your child to become sensitive to her environment.

Take an early morning hike with your child and talk about God's world—the flowers, trees, sky, people, and more. Let your child know that stewardship involves using every part of our life to glorify God. Remind him that all that we are and everything we own belongs to God, and we are to work for Him on earth. Read Matthew 25:14–30, and ask your child to think of ways he can glorify God with his money, time, talents, mind, and body.

The Christian Response

Psalm 24:1 says, "The earth is the Lord's and the fulness thereof" (RSV). In other words, we don't own our planet; we are taking care of it for God. Yes, we are His caretakers. In Genesis 2:15 we find that the Lord put man in the garden of Eden to, "till it and keep it" (RSV). To "keep" means to preserve and protect, to maintain its divinely termed "goodness."

Here are some ways you can educate your family about caring for God's earth.

Make it a family project to become informed about problems caused by current actions. Teach your children that plastic is not biodegradable. But it is recyclable! Along with filling the recycling bins with newspapers each week, encourage your child to include all plastic products—cola and ketchup bottles, plastic cartons, plastic boxes, and more.

When you make lunches for school or work, put food items in reusable containers instead of foil or plastic wrap.

Instead of tossing school papers that have been used, collect used paper and use the flip side for lists, drawing, doing math problems for homework, or for errand and grocery lists.

Don't forget glass and aluminum. Glass bottles and jars can also be recycled. Keep a special box for glass that will be made into "new" glass instead of filling up space at a landfill. Encourage your child to recycle all aluminum cans. Did you know that if you recycle just four aluminum cans, you will save enough electricity to run a television for sixteen hours?

Make children aware of their environment. Conserving electricity means that the power company doesn't have to produce as much. Challenge each family member to be responsible for turning off the lights in his or her bedroom plus one other room in the house. This ownership will help your children become more responsible.

A PARENT'S GOAL: LIVE YOUR FAITH

The greatest gift you can give to your child is to share your faith. Helping her share this faith through giving and helping the needy will add maturity to her developing spirituality. "Feet-to-faith" living is the ultimate response to a personal relationship with Jesus Christ.

Proverbs 22:6 teaches us to "Train children in the right way and when old, they will not stray." In our busy world, it is often difficult to give children the training necessary for Christian discipleship. But as we create an environment in our home for God's grace to be shared, with faith in Jesus Christ as the expected result, we will not only nurture their spirituality, but will also build strength in our children that will help them cope with adult years.

Christ believed in the principle that a small group of well-trained disciples could permeate a larger group in much the same way that a little yeast in the bread dough leavens the whole loaf (Luke 13:21). Jesus not only taught this principle, He put it into practice in the training of the twelve disciples. He invested Himself in an intimate, instructive, purposeful relationship with them. Through the course of a few years, He trained them by indelibly stamping their lives with a model of ministry they could not forget.[6]

As Christian parents, we also must indelibly stamp the young lives within our families. Our concern for our children must be so intimate, so full of selfless love, that they will *know* we are authentic. "Ye yourselves are taught of God to love one another" 1 Thessalonians 4:9 (KJV) tells us. Still, the questions remain: When do I show concern? How do I let my child know I am sincerely concerned for him?

Let's look at some ways parents can indelibly stamp lives in the family with the model of Christ's ministry:

- Put a love note in your child's lunch and write down your favorite love Scripture.

- Share Matthew 21:28–32. Talk about obedience.

- Rejoice that through Jesus Christ's coming, God is made known to all. Read Matthew 2:1–2 with your child.

- Volunteer to help with the children's or youth ministry at your church.

- Go for an evening walk with your children and talk about dreams of the future. Where do they see themselves ten years from now? Talk about God's plan for our lives.

- Read about the Good Samaritan and challenge your child to such actions. Read Luke 10:25–37 and talk about being helpful to others.

- You are your child's best teacher. Go to church together each week.

- Talk about Martin Luther King and the dream he had for all people. Teach your child that everyone is equal in God's eyes.

- Share your faith in Jesus with your child today. At what time in your life did He become real to you?

- Take time to give your child a giant bear hug—just because you love her. Read Luke 15:20 with your child.

- Talk about the meaning of the Lord's Supper. Read Matthew 26:26–30.

- Invite your pastor or child's Sunday school teacher to lunch.

- Openly forgive your child for any wrongdoing. Begin anew.

- Talk about Abraham Lincoln and prejudice. Share how this is a form of hatred.

- Write your child a love letter, telling him why he is special to you.

- Say an extra prayer for your child's teachers.

- Talk about your family's roots in the Christian faith. Read 2 Timothy 1:5.

- Share your spiritual growth with your child. Talk about your personal doubts and stumbling blocks and how God gives you strength.

- Join hands at dinner tonight and repeat the Lord's Prayer.

- Tell your child about your prayer and devotion time. Share how God reveals Himself to you.

- Discuss potential and doing one's best in life. Read Luke 5:27–32.

- Teach how making choices is difficult, especially for younger children. Read Joshua 23:14–15.

- Avoid majoring on the minors. What personal standards are most important in your family? (Respect, morals, obedience, abstinence, and love of God.)

- Encourage your child to develop his relationship with his grandparents. Call them after church or go visit.

- God calls us all to be witnesses to Jesus Christ. Share your faith with someone today.

- Pray for your child today. Read James 5:16.

- Revamp schedules to eat dinner as a family all week and share how God was revealed to you each day.

- Watch TV with your child. Are the values presented consistent with yours? Talk about this.

- More is caught than taught. Are you a loving adult role model?

- Tempers hot? Talk about peacemaking in the family. Read Matthew 5:9.

- Talk about fears with your child. Read Psalm 6:6–7.

- Is your child strong with peers? Help him memorize Psalm 31:24.

- Teens feel immortal. Read Mark 8:31–33 and 9:30–32.

- Doubting one's faith is normal. Read Job and talk about life's trials.

- Wipe out fear of failure. Read Isaiah 33:1–2.

- Sit outside with your child and watch the stars while talking about God's awesome love and power.

- Share Hebrews 13:14 and Galatians 3:19–20 and talk about sexuality and being a Christian.

- If your child is feeling low, read Romans 5:3 together.

- Trust cements the parent-child relationship. Think of ways to increase this.

- Purchase Scripture cards and put them on the kitchen table.

- Pray for patience. Rearing children can get anyone down. God can help.

- Don't let Sunday School and church be optional. Go with your child.

- Don't be quick to rescue a child from failure. Use it as a time to grow.

- Read aloud current news stories and discuss. What is the Christian response?

- Is your child overly critical of others? Read Luke 6:37.

- Talk about personal family values after church today.

- Share some of the family traditions you had when you were a child. Can you do these today?

- Love is easier said than done. Read Matthew 22:37–39.

Becoming Spiritual Soulmates with Your Child

In Philippians 4:13, Paul says, "I can do everything God asks me to with the help of Christ who gives me the strength and power" (TLB). Our Christian faith is a faith of hope. Realizing the possibility and promise in our lives is one of the keys to successful Christian living. Seeing the possibility in your child as you set goals for spiritual growth in the family can be exciting! The awesome power of God is limitless—if you come before Him with an attitude of anticipation, knowing that you are guiding your child in a spiritual awakening.

Becoming spiritual soulmates with your child depends on you—the parent. As you deepen your internal life, develop a spiritual attitude toward your daily actions, and use innovative tools to teach the Christian faith in your family, your child not only will experience a spiritual awareness, but also will grow in faith and understanding of our Lord Jesus Christ.

Spiritual Food for Thought

1. It's hard to love others in the midst of living such a hurried life. Take time each day this week and find a way to help someone else, either in your home, at work, or in your neighborhood or church. How did you feel after giving to someone else?

2. Random acts of kindness are unplanned and can be done for others anytime during the day. Using the list on pages 174–75, challenge your child to perform a random act of kindness for a sibling or friend each day this week. Take this

challenge personally and do one yourself at work or in the community each day.

3. Call a volunteer organization in your community to see if you and your child could help. Make plans to volunteer periodically with your child, and talk with your child about the good feelings we have when we reach out and help other people.

4. Does your family recycle regularly? Challenge your family to recycle and conserve energy in the home, and read to your children the conservation ideas on page 183. Put a chart in the kitchen, listing products such as paper, glass, and aluminum cans, and let your child check items off each day as she recycles these items.

5. We are all stewards of God's earth. Take a walk with your child and talk about ways you could improve your community. Challenge your child to become environmentally aware as he picks up litter and cares for God's planet.

Notes

INTRODUCTION

1. David Heller, *Talking to Your Child about God* (New York: Bantam Books, 1988), 6.

2. Carolyn Hoyt, "Giving Your Child a Spiritual Life" (*Parents*, February 1995), 95–99.

3. Heller, *Talking to Your Child about God*, 6.

4. "The Benefits of a Healthy Self-Esteem Are Evident," *ParentLife*, (November 1994), 20.

CHAPTER 1

1. Suzanne Johnson, *Christian Spiritual Formation in the Church and Classroom* (Nashville: Abingdon Press, 1989), 16.

2. Thomas Moore, *Care of the Soul* (New York: HarperCollins Publishers, 1992), xvi.

3. Princeton Religion Research Center, Emerging Trends (1995).

4. *ParentLife* (August 1994), 6.

5. Heller, *Talking to Your Child about God*, 7.

6. Leslie Krober, "Learning How to Change," *The Preacher's Magazine* (Dec./Jan./Feb. 1995), 65.

7. *Walking with Christ, Design for Discipleship* (Colorado Springs: Navpress, 1984), 5.

CHAPTER 2

1. *Pursuits* (12 February 1995), 59.

2. David M. Thomas, "What Every Family Needs: A Good Theology," *The Catholic World* (July/August 1993), 169.

3. John Westerhoff, *Will Our Children Have Faith?* (New York: The Seabury Press, 1976), 91–99.

4. Billy Graham, *Peace with God* (New York: Doubleday, 1953), 39–40.

5. "No Watered-Down Faith Message at this Teen Evangelism Gathering," *United Methodist Reporter* (January 3, 1995), 3.

6. Maxie Dunnam, *The Workbook of Intercessory Prayer* (Nashville: Upper Room Books, 1994), 16.

7. *Pursuit* (Oct./Nov./Dec. 1994), 109.

8. Elizabeth L. Reed, *Helping Children with the Mystery of Death* (Nashville: Abingdon, 1970), 25.

9. Delia Touchton Halverson, *Helping Your Teen Develop Faith* (Valley Forge, Pa.: Judson Press, 1988), 61.

10. William H. Willamon, *Pulpit Resource* (April, May, June 1995) Vol. 23, No. 2, Year C, 13.

11. *The Spirit-Filled Christian* (Navpress, 1984), 14.

12. John R.W. Stott, *Understanding the Bible* (London: Scripture Union, 1972), 183.

13. Debra Fulghum Bruce, *Making Memories That Count* (Missouri: Chrism, 1994), 36.

CHAPTER 3

1. Carolyn Hoyt, *Parents* (February 1995), 96.

2. "Hanging Tough with a 'No Fear' Generation" *The United Methodist Reporter* (Jan. 3, 1995), 2.

3. Graham, *Peace with God,* 177–78.

CHAPTER 4

1. O. Hallesby, *Prayer* (Minneapolis, Minn.: Augsburg, 1975), 35.

2. *Adult Bible Studies* (Nashville: Board of Discipleship) October 1990, 69.

CHAPTER 5

1. Maxie Dunnam, *The Workbook on Spiritual Disciplines* (Nashville: The Upper Room, 1984), 15.
2. Robert D. Foster, "Seven Minutes with God" (Colorado Springs: Navpress), 1.
3. Georgianna Summers, *Teaching as Jesus Taught* (Nashville: Discipleship Resources, 1983), 49.
4. Frances R. King, "Train Up a Child," *Living with Children* (April/May/June 1994), 42.

CHAPTER 6

1. Victor M. Parachin, "8 Ways to Grow Spiritually," *Keys to Christian Education* (Spring 1994), 6.
2. Jane Landreth, "Sensing God's World," *Keys to Christian Education* (Autumn 1994), 5.
3. Barbara Bolton, "Using All Five Senses," *Key to Christian Education* (Autumn 1994), 13.
4. Joan E. Cass, *Helping Children Grow Through Play* (New York: Schocken Books, 1973), 74.

CHAPTER 7

1. Lawrence Kohnberg and Carol Gilligan, "The Adolescent as Philosopher," *Twelve to Sixteen: Early Adolescence*, ed. Robert Coles, et al. (New York: W. W. Norton, 1972), 33.
2. Barbara Kantrowitz, "The Good, the Bad, and the Difference," *Newsweek* (special issue, 1991), 48.
3. David M. Thomas, "What Every Family Needs: A Good Theology," *The Catholic World* (July/August 1993), 170.
4. E. Kent Hayes, "How to be a Better Parent," *Redbook* (August 1990), 133.
5. "A Guide to Giving Children Values They Can Lean On," *Essence Communications* (1989, 64.
6. Kantrowitz, "The Good, the Bad, and the Difference," 48.
7. Crystal Trout Baker, "Thankfulness," *ParentLife* (November 1994), 42.
8. *Pursuits* (Oct./Nov./Dec. 1994), 98–99.

CHAPTER 8

1. David Veerman, "The World at Your Door," *Christian Parenting Today* (January/February 1995), 22–25.

2. Leslie Krober, "Living with a Purpose," *The Preacher's Magazine* (Dec./Jan./Feb. 1995), 59.

3. Frances Loftiss Carroll, *How to Talk with Your Children About God* (New York: Prentice Hall, 1985), 25.

4. *The World Is Not Enough* (California: Gospel Light Publications, 1986), 21.

CHAPTER 9

1. Delia Halverson, *How Do Our Children Grow?* (Nashville: Abingdon, 1993), 96.

2. Victor M. Parachin, "8 Ways to Grow Spiritually" *Keys to Christian Education* (Spring 1994), 6.

3. Victor M Parachin, *Grief Relief* (St. Louis: CBP Press, 1991), 27–34.

4. "Give Them Permission to Express Feelings," *Ladies' Home Journal* (March 1992), 50.

5. Robert V. Dodd, *When Someone You Love Dies* (Nashville: Abingdon, 1992), 11.

CHAPTER 10

1. Richard L. Dresselhaus, "Faith That Works," *Pentecostal Evangel* (March 19, 1995), 5.

2. James P. Comer, "Cultivating Spirituality," *Parents* (July 1992), 145.

3. Mary Lou Redding, "A Time to Act," *The Upper Room* (January/February 1995), 36.

4. Crystal Trout Baker, "Giving," *ParentLife* (Dec. 1994), 42.

5. "What to Do with Our Waste," *Newsweek* (1987), 57.

6. Win Arn, *The Pastor's Growth Handbook* (Pasadena: Church Growth Press, 1979), 29.